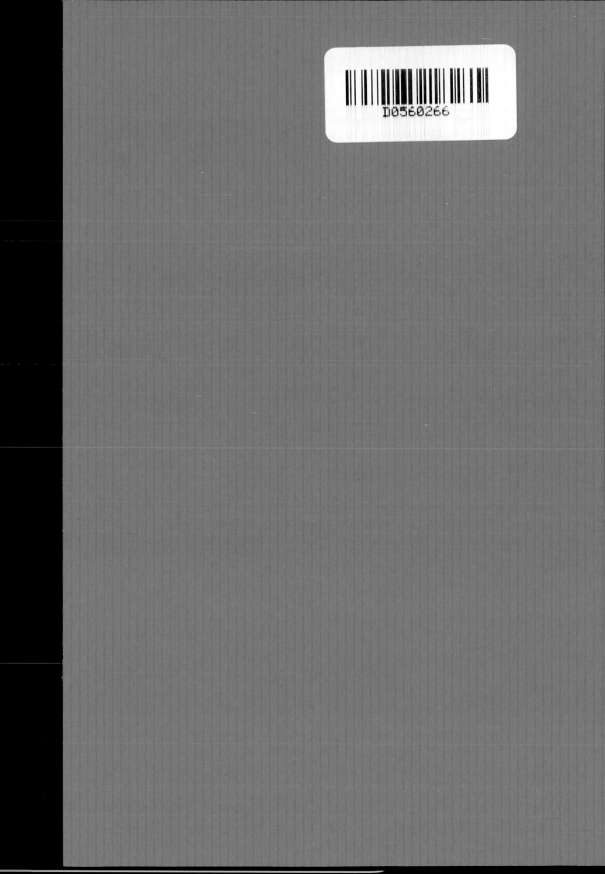

BLUEPRINTS
for a
SOLID MARRIAGE

FOCUS ON THE FAMILY®
RESOURCES

BLUEPRINTS
for a
SOLID
MARRIAGE

BUILD ✳ REMODEL ✳ REPAIR

DR. STEVE STEPHENS

TYNDALE HOUSE PUBLISHERS
Carol Stream, Illinois

Blueprints for a Solid Marriage
Copyright © 2006 by Dr. Erroll "Steve" Stephens
All rights reserved. International copyright secured.

ISBN-10: 1-58997-358-5
ISBN-13: 978-1-58997-358-9

A Focus on the Family book published by
Tyndale House Publishers, Carol Stream, Illinois 60188

TYNDALE is a registered trademark of Tyndale House Publishers, Inc. Tyndale's quill logo is a trademark of Tyndale House Publishers, Inc.

All Scripture quotations, unless otherwise indicated, are taken from the *Holy Bible, New International Version®*. NIV®. Copyright © 1973, 1978, 1984 by International Bible Society. Used by permission of Zondervan Publishing House. All rights reserved.

Scripture quotations marked (TLB) are taken from *The Living Bible* (paraphrase) copyright © 1971. Used by permission of Tyndale House Publishers, Inc., Carol Stream, Illinois 60188. All rights reserved.

Scripture quotations marked (MSG) are taken from *The Message* (paraphrase). Copyright © by Eugene H. Peterson 1993, 1994, 1995. Used by permission of NavPress Publishing Group.

The case examples presented in this book are fictional composites based on the author's clinical experience with hundreds of clients through the years. Any resemblance between these fictional characters and actual persons is coincidental.

No part of this publication may be reproduced, stored in a retrieval system, or transmitted in any form or by any means—electronic, mechanical, photocopy, recording, or otherwise—without prior permission of the publisher.

Editors: Mick Silva, Liz Duckworth, Mike Morrell
Cover design: Ron Kaufmann
Cover photo: copyright © by Jim Boorman/Getty Images. All rights reserved.
Back cover photo of floor: copyright © by iStockphoto.com. All rights reserved.

Library of Congress Cataloging-in-Publication Data
Stephens, Steve, 1954-
  Blueprints for a solid marriage : build, repair, remodel / Steve Stephens.
     p. cm. — (A focus on the family book)
  ISBN-13: 978-1-58997-358-9
  ISBN-10: 1-58997-358-5
  1. Marriage. 2. Family. I. Title. II. Series.
  HQ503.S695 2006
  646.7'8—dc22

                                              2005029215

Printed in the United States of America
1 2 3 4 5 6 7 8 9 /10 09 08 07 06

CONTENTS

Introduction

YOUR PERSONAL
WALK-THROUGH

"Unless the Lord builds a house,
the work of the builders is useless."
—King Solomon

I was glad to be home.

The church service was good, but now it was time to look at the newspaper and relax. I walked into the family room on a blue-sky Sunday afternoon and immediately knew something was wrong. My eyes were drawn to the center of the off-white brocaded ceiling. Then I saw a single drop of water fall soundlessly to the beige carpet below. I walked closer and saw it—the center of the ceiling was sagging. How could that happen?

I grabbed a bucket and pushed the blade of a pocketknife into the soggy sheetrock. Water rushed out and quickly filled half my bucket. Where is all this water coming from? I set the bucket beneath the sag, just in time to catch the next drip, and went upstairs in search of a renegade water source. The master bathroom above the family room looked safe: no broken pipes, no leaky faucets, no overflowing toilets or tubs. Everything looked in order. But something had to be wrong.

I measured off the room in my mind and determined that the toilet was directly above the saggy ceiling, and then I remembered that the toilet had been slightly unlevel ever since it had been replaced some three years before. I had almost entirely forgotten about it. I was going to fix it one of these days, but hadn't gotten to it yet. After all, it flushed, it was sealed, and there had been no noticeable leaks.

I called Dan, my I-can-fix-anything friend, and he came over. Together we pulled out my toilet, and there was the leak. We then went downstairs and cut a hole in the family room ceiling. What we saw was not pretty— a layer of mold covered the top side of the ceiling sheetrock. We cut an eight-foot by twelve-foot hole in the ceiling to remove all the mold.

"What have you done to our house?" Tami asked when she came home.

"Just fixing a little leak." I tried to smile.

For the next 45 days we had a great view from our family room sofa of the upstairs floor joists and our master bath plumbing. By then the toilet was resealed, the sheetrock replaced, the ceiling replastered. All it needed was a little repair and today everything looks great.

Your house is a bit like your marriage: Every marriage needs a periodic repair and remodel. Even the best marriages, like the best houses, need some work every once in a while. The sad thing is that most couples take better care of their house than their marriages. If you had committed to keep your house "Till death do us part," how would you treat it? Would you ignore:

- sweeping the floors,
- fixing the leak in the ceiling,
- washing the windows,
- scrubbing the toilets,
- changing the light bulbs,
- and other small, routine repairs?

Even the most fantastic houses lose their appeal and excitement if they are not properly maintained. They grow stale and dingy. They start looking a bit run-down. If you let things go too long, you might be tempted to just sell the place and start looking for something new. Or complain to the neighbors about how things aren't as good as they used to be. Or maybe just stare at the cobwebs on the ceilings and shake your head at the filthy carpets. Instead of these dismal options, both houses and marriages benefit when you perform routine maintenance checks and determine what needs to be repaired, remodeled, or just cleaned up.

Sometimes you need a repair.

Things need to be fixed so they work the way they should. Unfortunately things in a relationship get broken over time. Maybe it's normal wear and tear. Maybe it's natural causes like termites or dry rot. Maybe it's breakage or neglect because you haven't treated things as carefully as needed.

Sometimes you need a remodel.

Things just don't look as good as they could. You might need more space or wish to reconfigure the space you have. Maybe you wish to update or upgrade a room. For whatever reason, you determine that some improvements will make your situation more efficient, more comfortable, more attractive, or more fulfilling.

Sometimes you just need to clean up.

Shelves need to be dusted and walls need to be washed. Rooms aren't in terrible shape, but they don't look as nice and shiny as they once did. Accessories need to be straightened up and the garbage needs to be taken out; it may be creating a bad odor or collecting bugs or overflowing into the rest of the house.

Every house and every marriage needs a walk-through at least once a year to see what condition it is in. Even before you wed, it is a good idea to keep these things in mind. Think of it as a "home inspection" for the house the two of you are about to move into. As you walk through your relationship, discuss what you like, what you don't like, and what sort of work might need to be done. Here are 12 areas to consider:

1. The entryway: commitment projects
   Knowing what love and relationship is really all about
2. The closets: emotional projects
   Being in touch with each other's feelings
3. The kitchen: practical projects
   Tackling everyday chores as a team
4. The dining room: social projects
   Connecting with people who enrich your relationship
5. The family room: recreational projects
   Finding the fun and laughter of life together
6. The study: intellectual projects
   Sharing new thoughts, ideas, and opinions
7. The hallway: conflict projects
   Resolving differences with respect
8. The safe room: crisis projects
   Pulling close during challenges and difficulties
9. The patio: aesthetic projects
   Enjoying the beauty that surrounds you, together
10. The master bedroom: sexual projects
    Making touch and intimacy a way of strengthening your relationship
11. The addition: future projects
    Dreaming and planning about tomorrow
12. The foundation: spiritual projects
    Connecting with God and His purpose for life

A marriage walk-through allows you to evaluate your relationship and make it all that it can be. For those of you who have been married for a while, this helps you recapture the joy and excitement you had at the first. But the potential this walk-through holds is even better than that: The longer you are married, the more potential depth, sensitivity, and experience you are able to add. As long as you take proper care of your marriage, it will get better and better.

Seven years after Tami and I got married, we built a wonderful house. It was clean, fresh, and new. It was great. But over the past 13 years, our dream house has been lived in.

- Our dishwasher broke.
- Our carpets wore out.
- Our gutters filled with mud.
- Our family room got dry rot.
- Our walls became dingy.

However, Tami and I have regularly taken care of home improvement. Our house is now better than it was when we first built it. In the beginning our walls were all white; now they are full of all sorts of color. Over the years we have improved, fixed, and upgraded our house. We have added a room, built a cobblestone patio, upgraded our lighting fixtures, and turned a patch of dry, hard dirt into a lush, landscaped yard. Our house gets better every year, but it takes work. It's not easy, but it is certainly worth it. In every house, there are always projects. If you can't find any, you either aren't looking or aren't growing.

Tami and I have been married 22 years, and each year things have gotten better and better. We are both so glad we don't have the same struggles that we did our first year. All 12 areas of our marriage have improved, some naturally and some through intentional effort. We have had our fair share of repairs, remodels, and cleanups. Yet without these "home improvements" even the best relationships risk falling apart.

Too many couples divorce.

Too many couples live in relationships that are dissatisfying, disappointing, and at least partially dead. This doesn't have to happen. A regular walk-through alerts you to potential difficulties, shows you what must be dealt with next, and helps both of you to understand each other's needs and expectations. Walk-throughs can be fun. They are also one of the smartest things you will ever do.

If your needs aren't being met, don't give up.

If you are hurt or unhappy or disappointed, don't give up.

If you are bored and the excitement is gone, don't give up.

If you are considering divorce, don't give up.

If you can't even see the use in trying, don't give up.

If you wish you could start fresh with someone new, don't give up.

Please don't give up!

You can have a great marriage.

No marriage is perfect, but every marriage can be improved. Marriages fall apart because needs are not met. All 12 areas of your house represent a particular need in your marriage. Some of these might be major needs and some minor, but all of them are important. The ones which are most important to him might not be the most important to her. Yet the more areas of your house you feel good about, the better you feel about the whole house. Still, one damaged, dirty, or dry-rotted area can spread to adjoining areas, and soon it may feel like the whole house has deteriorated and depreciated in value.

Marriages, like houses, are meant to increase in value; when we discover their value is decreasing, we frequently fall into one of two dangerous patterns:

- Passivity: Things are bad, but there is nothing I can do about it. So I had better just face reality and accept the situation the way it is.
- Panic: Things are bad, but there is nothing I can do about it. So I had better end the relationship and get out of this situation as fast as I can.

There is a third more positive and productive option: home improvement.

It might not be quick or clever, but it works. Do you want a healthy marriage? Then get together and walk through the 12 areas of your relationship. Some of these areas look great and are just the way you like them. But there are other areas that need some work. Don't panic or get passive; simply set up your projects. Here are a few initial questions:

What areas need the most work?

When do you start?

What are your expectations?

How are you going to get started?

What materials are needed?

Can you do it yourselves or do you need some outside help?

So, are we ready? If you want to recapture the love you once had and upgrade all you currently have, let's go. Grab your partner's hand, open the front door, and let's begin your marriage walk-through. As you imagine your home improvements you will be on your way to making your relationship:

- stronger,
- deeper,
- warmer,
- better,
- and built to last a lifetime.

❋ ❋ ❋

Imagine yourself as a living house. God comes in to rebuild that house. At first, perhaps you can understand what He is doing. He is getting the drains right and stopping the leaks in the roof and so on: you knew that those jobs needed doing and so you are not surprised. But presently He starts knocking the house about in a way that hurts abominably and does not seem to make sense. What on earth is He up to? The explanation is that He is building quite a different house from the one you thought of—throwing out a new wing here, putting on an extra floor there, running up towers, making courtyards. You thought you were going to be made into a decent little cottage: but He is building a palace. He intends to come and live in it Himself.

—C. S. Lewis, *Mere Christianity*

1

THE ENTRYWAY
Commitment Projects

You start with the door. Ours is white with leaded glass at the top and a welcome mat in front of it. You knock or ring the doorbell and are invited into our entryway. This is where everything starts.

In some homes you take off your shoes or boots here and line them against a wall. Other entryways have a coatrack, an umbrella tree, or a table for the mail.

When I was eight years old, my parents bought a large house without an entryway. The front door just opened into the living room. This must have bothered my dad, because a year or two later he created an entryway. He set aside a six-foot by five-foot area inside the door and covered the floor with slate. Then he put a fancy light fixture in the ceiling and added a built-in planter to separate the entrance from the rest of the house.

What you see when you first walk through the front door tells you a lot about how a couple treats and even feels about their house.
- What are the colors?
- What items are on the walls?

- Do things appear to be in good repair?
- How does it smell?
- How clean?
- How cluttered?
- What is your first impression?

When you first walk into our house you'll see a chair, a quilt, a vase with fresh-cut flowers, and a wall full of family pictures. Tami has created an atmosphere that is simple, relaxing, and welcoming.

Entryways are important. They are the beginning. Yet in our fast-paced lives, we frequently ignore the entryway. We rush through the garage door or the back door. We forget the entryway, and this is a big mistake. This area might appear small or relatively purposeless, but it is very important for it sets the atmosphere for the whole house.

This area represents the commitments of marriage. They are what get you started on the right track. If the commitments are ignored or broken, you will have a drafty house. Several years ago my front door frame was knocked off-kilter and the door lost its seal. I had to slam it hard and it still wouldn't close properly. That winter the northeast winds blew hard against my door, stealing the heat of our house and creating drafts. Tami complained about the chill and the children wore sweaters to stay warm. In the meantime our heating bill became unreasonable. Finally, I hired a repairman who worked on the frame and replaced the seals. Now the door closes tight, the drafts are gone, and my heating bill doesn't create panic. Commitment is the seal that takes care of the drafts in your marriage and keeps your relationship warm.

So let's open your front door, step into your entryway, and look at commitment.

True Commitment

"I don't believe in commitment," said the attractive 20-something as she shifted in her chair. "All you do is give away your heart and then get hurt. I'd much rather live together for a year and see if it works. Then maybe we'll get married. If that doesn't work, we'll just shake hands, say good-bye, and go our separate ways."

No commitment.

No hurt.

No hassle.

"Why bother?" I asked.

"What?" she said with a look of surprise.

"Why not just say good-bye today and go your separate ways?"

"But I love him and sooner or later we want to get married."

"With your philosophy toward relationships, I guarantee that your marriage will never last."

"Why not?" she asked, genuinely perplexed.

"Because commitment is everything," was my simple reply.

Commitment is the core of trust and trust is the core of every worthwhile relationship. If I trust you, we can build a friendship. If I can't trust you, we have nothing.

Getting married involves a commitment—one of the most important commitments you will ever make. This is a turning point in your life. It is opening the door to the greatest test of character you will ever face. You stand before friends and relatives. You hold the hands of your future and say those unforgettable words:

In sickness and health;

For richer or poorer;

For better or worse;

Till death do us part.

Now, do you have the courage and character to live those words? These are not meaningless, off-the-top-of-your-head, throwaway words. These words constitute a sacred vow. Marriage vows are made to:

- God,
- your spouse,
- yourself,
- your family,
- your friends,

- your community,
- and everyone who really cares about you.

At that moment you committed yourself—your heart, your will, your body. You committed 100 percent of who you are, no holding back.

But how can you commit to a future which might not turn out as you expect? What if something horrible happens? What if your world flips upside down? What if your beloved turns bad or lazy or abusive or fat?

What if you meet someone with whom you are more perfectly and passionately matched?

What if I said: "None of this matters!"

I once met an old veteran who had fought in WWII. "I'd rather die than break my word," he said.

"Isn't that sort of drastic?"

"No, sir," he said. "Your word is your reputation and without a reputation you are nothing."

Times sure have changed.

Hardly anybody keeps their word anymore.

Vows are broken.

People are broken.

Commitment need not fall by the wayside, however. Life is going to be tough; that's just the way it is. But there is hope. Real commitment can work.

"Sure," said a friend. "Now commitment is a synonym for hell or purgatory."

Commitment is only miserable if you make it that way.

When two people get married there are seven commitments that are absolutely critical.

Commitment to Oneness

The Bible says that the two joined in marriage shall become one. You are both on the same team. You either win as a team or lose as a team. You laugh together and cry together. What hurts your spouse should hurt you. What excites your spouse should excite you.

It's like a three-legged race: If you've got the rhythm, you move. If you are out of step, you fall.

When you are working as one, you do nothing that would hurt, belittle, discourage, frustrate, or limit your spouse. In fact, you do just the opposite: You do everything within your power to heal, compliment, encourage, build up, and strengthen your spouse.

Whatever you do for your partner, you are in fact doing for yourself. That's what oneness means. You do what's best for the relationship, not just what's good for the individuals. Thus a sacred "we" is formed, and in every circumstance the "me" submits to the "we." The "me" is not lost. It is just that as the "me" strengthens the "we," the "we" strengthens the "me." And so the two are truly one.

Oneness means sharing, and the more you share, the more you become one. So share your feelings, thoughts, experiences, and laughter.

You can even share your pain, needs, worries, and dreams. But in the midst of the stress and a hectic pace, don't forget to share your love.

Commitment to Positive Communication

When you go to a restaurant you can tell who has been married a long time. It's those couples who sit face-to-face and rarely talk to each other. Sometimes they don't even look at each other.

Too tired.

Too angry or hurt.

Too bored or lonely or disconnected.

Something has gone wrong; the words that once brought understanding and laughter and romance have run dry. Words are the lifeblood of healthy relationships. You give them and receive them. They inform and comfort and compliment and connect.

Committed couples communicate.

Positive communication is the top predictor of a strong marriage. Two people who wish to have a real relationship share their thoughts and feelings, their hopes and fears. They listen carefully and respond with respect. They don't belittle or assume the worst or call names. Instead they encourage and compliment and look for ways to build up each other. They ask questions and allow for individual differences—differences of opinion, preference, perspective, and even communication.

Communication isn't always easy, but it is always worth it. Joshua Harris, in his book *Boy Meets Girl,* provides the following principles for authentic communication:

- Communication problems are usually heart problems.
- Your ears are your most important communication tools.
- Good communication doesn't happen by accident.
- The absence of conflict doesn't equal good communication.
- Motive is more important than technique.

Commitment to Quality Time

Gary Chapman lists quality time as one of five "love languages." The more intentional and deliberate the time spent together, the closer you feel to one another. "How long has it been since you've had quality time together?" I asked one young couple.

They both laughed—nervously.

"We have three kids," she explained.

"I have a demanding job and I'm working for a big promotion," he added.

"So how long?" I insisted.

"Two years," he said.

"And how long has your marriage been stuck in its current rut?"

"Two years," she said.

That night the two climbed out of their rut and had some quality time. It probably saved their marriage.

How can you be sure you have the quality time your marriage needs?

Make it a top priority to spend time together doing things you both enjoy. Have a good conversation, a good walk, or just a good time. Life gets crazy and hectic and moves way too fast. If you don't schedule quality time, it doesn't happen. So pull out your calendar and write it down. Set aside a time alone, without distractions, where the two of you can really connect. This needs to be an oasis from the external, time where you don't talk about kids, finances, work, or difficulties. Time where you can relax and develop your friendship on a deeper level.

Here are a few ideas for your quality time:
- Cuddle on the couch.
- Dream new dreams together.
- Take a drive.
- Read a book to each other.
- Explore someplace new.
- Talk about your passions.
- Meet at a coffee shop.
- Go on a real romantic date.

Commitment to Growth

Make every year better than the last. Tami will tell you that our first year of marriage was the most difficult. Since then, it has kept getting better and better. But it takes work. Any endeavor that's truly worthwhile takes effort and commitment. If you want good grades or a good job, you put in the time. If you want a great garden, you plant, weed, water, and fertilize. These actions, with a little help from the weather and the One who controls the weather, cause the plants to grow. Tami has a great garden. She takes care of it, and from spring through fall it produces a diverse variety of food and flowers. She takes care of the garden, and the garden takes care of her.

So be committed to the growth of your marriage and you will be blessed. Do not focus on changes you wish your spouse would make. Instead, do whatever you can to be the best husband or wife you can be. Learn what your spouse's needs are and meet them. Find out what it takes to have a good marriage and do it. Whether you are a reader or not, read at least one book on marriage each year. Go to a relationship seminar, a marriage encounter, or a couples' retreat.

Discover what you do that offends, frustrates, or hurts your spouse, and stop doing it. Listen closely to the things your partner has asked from you for so long, those things you ignore, put off, or just refuse to do. Ask yourself why you haven't done these things and unless you have a really good reason, do them. As you practice this loving attentiveness, you will find that you grow deeper and closer to your mate. You also grow more committed.

Commitment to Faithfulness

"Never take off your wedding ring."

"Why?" I asked my grandmother.

"Because it reminds you and everybody else that you're married."

That was pretty good advice.

Too many people seem to have forgotten that they are married and what that really means: You are taken. You belong to your spouse and to nobody else. Look at your wedding ring and remember the day it first slipped on your finger. If you're engaged, reflect on the ramifications of what you're preparing for.

The ring symbolizes your total commitment to that one special person. So why visit a chat room, flirt with a coworker, or let your mind go where it shouldn't go?

You are married and married people are faithful to each other. That means you don't let anyone—real or imaginary—get between you and your spouse. You guard your heart and avoid situations that might tempt you. Be careful where you look, what you say, and how emotionally close you get to the opposite sex. Never allow emotional or sexual needs that should be met by your partner be met by someone else—even if that someone else is kinder, cuter, smarter, or more understanding than your spouse. A faithful spouse refuses to be tempted by cybersex or pornography, fantasies or affairs, intimate friendships or an inappropriate touch.

They are 100 percent emotionally and sexually committed no matter what. Here are a few ways to protect your faithfulness:

- Wear your wedding ring.
- Don't flirt.
- Don't be alone with the opposite sex.
- Avoid secrets.
- Let your spouse know the wheres, whens, whos, and whys of your schedule.
- Run all gifts or favors to the opposite sex past your spouse.
- Talk positively about your mate.
- Always carry each other's picture.
- Flee areas of romantic and/or sexual temptations.
- Remember the great times you have had together.
- Never look at pornography.
- Recognize how much unfaithfulness would hurt your spouse, your children, and your reputation.
- Don't discuss sexual issues with members of the opposite sex unless within a medical/psychological setting.
- Pray for your marriage.

Commitment to Honesty

"Should I tell my wife?"

"Why wouldn't you?" I asked the CEO of a multimillion-dollar company.

"She might lose respect for me and it could seriously damage our marriage."

"If you don't tell her the truth, she will lose respect for you." Ultimately the truth is always discovered. Sooner or later it comes to the surface. If you don't tell your spouse, he or she will ultimately find out and feel deceived by your dishonesty. Truth is basic to trust. Lies and secrets and silence create deep cracks in your relationship that can break apart the best of marriages.

The two of you are one and within one there need be nothing hidden. Secrets between a husband and wife will sooner or later get you into trouble. The first problem is that secrets are progressive. You start with one, and then you need another to cover up the first. And then another and another and another.

A second problem is that secrets remove you from accountability. When your spouse knows all, you tend to be more responsible and less prone to fall into temptation. Your partner protects you from your weaknesses and you do the same for your partner. This can only be done in an atmosphere of honesty and trust. Therefore, before you do anything in the least bit questionable, ask yourself:

- Do I feel comfortable telling my spouse everything I'm about to do?
- How will my partner respond to this?
- Will this activity distance us or bring us closer together?

When honesty and love is the currency, a marriage is bound to be rich. I believe in a commitment to total honesty, but there are three exceptions to this rule. I encourage individuals to be very cautious about sharing:

- information that is both hurtful and unnecessary;
- information about any sexual partners you may have had from before you met each other;
- if there has been an affair, information about the specific details of the sexual encounter. (To share this data potentially creates visual images that can make it difficult for the offended party to heal.)

Commitment to the Long Haul

A young couple who was struggling through their first year of not-so-wedded-bliss asked me how long I'd been married.

"Sixteen years," was my reply.

"What?" the wife asked with a look of shock.

"Sixteen years," I repeated.

"You've got to be kidding!" she said in amazement.

"Sixteen years, and it gets better every year."

"I've never met anybody who's stayed married that long and still likes it," was her response.

What does "till death do us part" mean anymore? Couples marry and divorce and marry someone new with such regularity that it has become the norm. Divorce doesn't shock anyone anymore. It's just a part of life. We have to realize that this is tragically wrong, unhealthy, and extremely dangerous. Divorce damages your children, family, and community. It scars your emotions, beliefs, and spirit. It traps you in a position of selfish immaturity. One famous psychologist says he does not believe in divorce because terminating a relationship blocks personal growth. He says that the tough times in marriage develop character. But we live in a time when comfort takes priority over character.

Tami and I have made an agreement with our kids that we will not divorce. We stood in our kitchen and held hands with our three children and promised that we would stay together for the long haul. There are at least 10 benefits of a healthy long-haul relationship.

- It teaches love.
- It develops patience.
- It conquers loneliness.
- It lengthens life.
- It nurtures children.
- It models responsibility.
- It enriches memories.
- It builds character.
- It passes on heritage.
- It pleases God.

Wrap Up

Without commitment no marriage will last. In the last third of the twentieth century, our culture tried a massive social experiment that was a miserable failure. People tried "free" love, "open" marriage, "no-fault" divorce, and "serial" monogamy. None of it worked. Millions of people were left scarred and broken. A generation has grown up not understanding that commitment is basic to marriage.

It is time to stop this stupid game.

It is time to grow up and build a real marriage—a marriage with good days and bad, with boredom and excitement, frustration and fun, hurt and joy. Marriage is a mixed bag, but in the end its benefits far outweigh its difficulties. A committed marriage takes maturity, confidence, and courage.

But a committed marriage is worth it. What it lacks in comfort, it makes up for in character. And character does matter.

Entryway Projects

1. Talk to your spouse about what commitment really means.
   - Which of the seven commitments is the most important to you?
   - Which is the hardest?
   - Why?

2. Make a vow to never threaten divorce. (Write it down, sign it, frame it, and hang it in your bedroom.)

3. Ask each other for one thing you'd like that would help you have a better marriage. Then do it.

4. Go on a date twice per month. (She plans the first date and he plans the second. Repeat the sequence each month.)

5. Read at least one book on marriage or relationships every year.

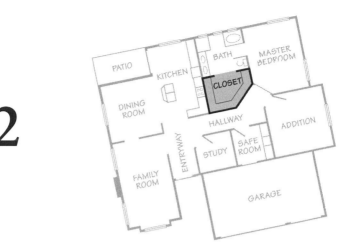

2

THE CLOSETS
Emotional Projects

Tami believes the more closets one has, the better.

I don't even think about closets.

Before we were married, I bought a cozy bungalow which had been built in 1902. It had a lot of character, but it only had two very small closets. When we got married, she quickly let me know that this was not adequate. I tried to reassure her by reminding her that the house had a basement in which we could store anything that would not fit in the closets. Somehow, this was not an acceptable solution; Tami wanted more closets.

So when we drew up the blueprints for our current house, Tami penciled in a lot of closets—and they weren't dinky, little closets. In our house we now have closets galore. We have a coat closet, a game closet, a linen closet, a food closet, and three storage closets. Each bedroom has a large clothes closet, especially the master bedroom.

But now I have a problem with closets. Somehow they become catchalls for all sorts of stuff. Our coat closet right next to the entryway is the most notorious culprit. Not long ago I gathered up the courage to explore what it held, and there was a lot more than just coats. I found books, a camera, a box of photographs, children's toys, umbrellas, earmuffs, gloves, hats, tablecloths, school papers, baseball bats, and several boxes of unknown content. As I talk to people about their closets, I usually hear words like *stuffed, unorganized,* and *overflowing.*

I love to clean out our closets. I get a certain glee out of throwing away what is no longer needed, donating unused items to Goodwill or simply organizing the clutter. Twice a year Tami goes through our master bedroom closet and sorts through our clothes. She points to each item and asks:

- Does it fit?
- Is it in style?
- Do I like it?
- Have I worn it in the last year?

If the answer to any of these questions is no, there is a good probability that the item will disappear. Last week my son Dusty decided to clean out our game closet. He reorganized everything, placing all the pieces of the games together and getting rid of all the puzzles that had missing pieces. Suddenly we could find what we wanted and didn't discover halfway through playing a game that crucial pieces were lost.

Every once in a while, a relationship needs to look at its emotional closets. Certain things need to be gotten rid of, other things need to be fixed. Sometimes things just need to be reorganized and placed where they can be found more easily. A messy closet can contaminate other areas of marriage. Too often we just stuff things that we don't know what to do with into a closet. If this continues over time, the emotional closet will reach a point where it can't handle anything more. At that point it bursts open and emotions are thrown all over our house.

If you don't deal with your emotions, sooner or later something will explode. That explosion could destroy a once beautiful house or a once wonderful marriage.

Emotional Togetherness

"The loneliness is killing me," cried Suzie. "My heart aches, but what makes it so painful is that James doesn't even seem to notice how much I hurt."

So I asked James, "What is happening with your wife?"

"Nothing," he said with a shrug of his shoulders. "Sometimes she keeps to herself and is a little moody, but that's just the way women are. She's fine."

"But she's not," I told James. "She hurts so bad that she's thinking about leaving you."

"No, that can't be. It just can't be."

Why was James having such a hard time dealing with Suzie's emotions? Part of the problem was that he didn't know how to tune in to her emotional wavelength.

You both are full of emotions. Some people are expressive with their feelings; they show their colors without anyone asking. If they are sad, angry, or happy, you know it. Others keep their feelings hidden; their poker faces don't even give a hint as to what lies within. But whether obvious or not, emotions are what move you and make you alive. Without them, relationships would have no spark, pizzazz, or true intimacy. Just two people connecting as brain and body. Feelings are what drive you deeper and closer. Feelings are what caused you to first consider marriage and feelings are what later tempt couples to throw in the towel when things get rough. Emotions are at times irrational and confusing, running the gamut from ecstasy to despair. Some days you embrace them, other days you curse them. Without feelings life would be flat and colorless; with them life is sometimes much too intense.

Emotional togetherness is one of the most neglected areas of marriage. It requires that you know your emotions and are honest about your hurts. Emotional togetherness means you are willing to open your vulnerability to your partner. It also requires that your spouse be willing to do the same.

Emotional togetherness involves four of the most challenging and rewarding steps you will ever take.

Emotional Awareness

To truly connect with your spouse, you need to know where he or she is emotionally. If your spouse is worried, you need to connect differently than when he or she is angry. And if your partner is happy, you connect in still a different way. Awareness is like taking a person's pulse: It tells you what's going on inside and it's easy to do once you know how.

How do you develop emotional awareness?

Really look.

Too often we don't even see what's right in front of us. It's like looking at a picture that has a hidden image in it. At first you can't see the secret shape. But after studying the picture carefully, it suddenly appears and you wonder how you could have missed something so obvious.

Your partner's emotional pulse is displayed in hundreds of visual clues, even if he or she is trying to keep it secret. The symptoms are evident, if you are observant. Study the body language. It's all there, for emotions seep from the body like cold water sweats from a glass on a hot summer's day. Some of the physical cues are:

- Curve of mouth
- Focus of eyes
- Twitches and tics
- Color of complexion
- Type of breathing
- Level of energy
- Shoulder/neck tension
- General restlessness
- Speed of walk
- Tilt of the head
- Tightness of the jaw
- Hard swallowing
- Biting lip
- Furrowed brow
- Grinding teeth
- Hand gestures
- Facial expression
- Posture

• Body language
• Foot movement

Really listen.
Listening is hard work, but it also provides another key to a person's emotional pulse. But don't just listen to the words.

Listen beneath,

between,

behind the words.

A song is more than just the words. There is pacing and phrasing, melody and music. The same song sung by a polished soprano orchestrated with a flute and soft piano sounds quite different when sung by a scratchy bass voice competing with driving drums and a screaming electric guitar. The emotional pulse is different, although in most situations the difference is a bit more subtle.

Slow down and listen. Hear the tune, the volume, the attitude, the speed, the type of words. What is the emotion behind the words? It is there—sometimes subtle, sometimes obvious. It is like trying to identify what musical instruments are playing your favorite song. The more practiced the ear, the more you hear.

Identify.
A furrowed brow and a trembling lip combined with a pause and hard swallow tells you something very important. Then your spouse blinks away a tear just before it falls.

What is your spouse telling you?

There are hundreds of emotions and a thousand gradations of each. Yet many of us are not good at identifying what we feel, let alone what a spouse is feeling. Here are 14 basic emotions that can serve as a beginning for taking both your and your spouse's emotional pulse.

	High	Moderate	Low
Anger	___	___	___
Attraction	___	___	___

Boredom	___	___	___
Contentment	___	___	___
Curiosity	___	___	___
Disgust	___	___	___
Exhaustion	___	___	___
Fear	___	___	___
Guilt	___	___	___
Loneliness	___	___	___
Playfulness	___	___	___
Sadness	___	___	___
Shock	___	___	___
Tension	___	___	___

Look into the face, listen to the voice, and you can identify the state of the heart. Now you know what makes your spouse move and what motivates him or her. You have your partner's emotional pulse and, at that moment, the most intimate, revealing, and vulnerable connection with his or her soul. Those who know how to handle the heart and soul have discovered a togetherness to be envied by all.

Emotional Analysis

Looking inside is difficult and sometimes painful. Emotional awareness often leads to dark and frightening trails that wander through disturbing lands you try hard to suppress. Yet your dark side is a reality. Honesty teaches humility as you discover the truth of the prophet Jeremiah when he said, "The heart is deceitful above all things" (Jeremiah 17:9).

As you show courage and integrity in understanding your heart—its secrets and shames, its insecurities and sensitivities, its passions and possibilities—you finally plunge beneath the well-crafted mask of civility and appearance.

Now you can be honest. At times you are irrational. At times you are mean and cruel. This is not a justification; it is simply reality. Do not embrace your dark side, but accept it. As you accept it in yourself, you can accept it in your spouse. And then you are in a position to analyze your emotional history, needs, and triggers.

History shapes you.

Your past—good, bad, and ugly—has shaped who you are today. Lori was sexually abused by an uncle; today she mistrusts men. Adam came from a loud and violent home, and now he withdraws whenever his wife gets intense. Felicity's father left the family for another woman. Twenty years later, whenever her husband glances at an attractive female, Felicity has a panic attack. History leaves its impact on each individual and every marriage. Share with your spouse your greatest traumas and hurts. Talk about your childhood tears and fears and joys. As you understand each other's history, you begin to understand who you both really are.

Needs differ.

The fears, traumas, and deprivations of childhood leave emotional scars on the adult. These scars surface as emotional needs that scream to be met, and you most often look to your partner for these needs to be met or at least affirmed.

Knowing your spouse's emotional needs is one of the most important tasks you will perform in your marriage. Be a student of your lover. Notice, study, gather your data, and do your best to meet his or her needs. Be your spouse's greatest cheerleader and comforter.

Everybody's needs are different. Five common relational needs are best described in Gary Chapman's book *The Five Love Languages*. They are:
- words of affirmation,
- gifts,
- physical touch,
- acts of service,
- quality time.

Which of these is your partner's greatest need? How frequently would he or she like you to meet this need? When is the last time you actually met it?

Know your triggers.

Our emotional history leaves needs, but it also leaves triggers. These triggers are a direct link to your emotional history. Any strong reaction—whether hurt, anger, or fear—has its roots in the past.

When Tony lost his high-paying job of eight years, he wasn't worried. He decided to take a few weeks off to relax and reflect on occupational opportunities. But one afternoon Cyndie came home from her work to find Tony unshaven, unbathed, and watching cartoons on television.

She hit the ceiling.

"You lazy, good-for-nothing bum," she screamed. "I work hard all day and you do nothing, absolutely nothing. I thought you loved me. I thought you were going to take care of me," she burst into sobs. "You will never find a job. We've worked hard for this house and now we won't even be able to make the mortgage payments."

What just happened?

This couple is financially secure and Tony is a hard worker. So why is Cyndie so upset?

Her fear is triggered.

She came from a family where her father had difficulty holding a job and they were frequently evicted from houses because they couldn't pay the rent. At times they didn't even have enough to eat. An insecurity and fear was built into Cyndie that she will never forget.

We all have triggers.

It works this way: An external sensory event—a sight, sound, smell, taste, or touch—triggers an unpleasant or uncomfortable memory. Then you react with a strong emotion that throws you into the classic fight-or-flight syndrome.

So know your triggers and manage your reactions. Some potential triggers are:

- tone of voice,
- attitudes,
- facial expressions,
- lack of respect,

- finances,
- alcohol,
- expectations,
- power and control,
- sexuality,
- perceived abandonment, rejection, or neglect.

Be aware of your partner's sensitivities and try not to trigger them. But if you do, don't get defensive. Stay calm. Communicate love and show that you are committed to emotional togetherness.

Emotional Articulation

Feelings are a mirror to your soul. If you are an extrovert, you might feel at ease expressing and talking about your emotions. But if you are an introvert, you probably hold your feelings in and find it uncomfortable talking about them.

God made everybody unique. Some speak openly and easily about their innermost feelings. Others struggle and strain to provide even a hint of what lies within. But if you cannot or will not speak about your feelings with your spouse, emotional intimacy will be elusive and every other type of togetherness will suffer.

So how do you become emotionally articulate?

You open your mouth, open your heart, and take a risk.

Name it.

Every night Jean and Michael sat face-to-face on their queen-sized bed and talked. Holding hands they looked into each other's eyes, admitting whatever stirred below the surface.

"Today I felt lonely and scared," she said.

Michael asked questions and listened patiently. "How long have you felt this? What triggered it? Where do you think this feeling came from? What would you like from me that might help?"

Then Michael talked about how angry he had felt earlier that day and how embarrassed he was about this emotion. Jean listened and helped him explore how he felt. When he finished, she hugged him and thanked him for his honesty.

Sound sappy?

Maybe. But it doesn't matter.

The issue is that it works.

Michael smiled. "I feel so free."

Jean ran her fingers through his hair. "I feel a lot closer to Michael than before our talk and I certainly understand him a lot more."

Jean and Michael learned how to name their feelings clearly and concisely. They both took responsibility for their emotions without blaming, defending, or minimizing what they felt.

You feel what you feel.

Name it and talk about it.

Is it easy?

No!

Is it comfortable?

No!

Is it embarrassing?

Sometimes.

Will it bring you closer to each other?

Yes!

Respect it.

"Why won't he open up and share his feelings?"

I've heard this question a thousand times and my response is usually the same. "Maybe he doesn't feel safe."

For her to be vulnerable, you need to truly listen and try to understand. For him to open up, you must be willing to respect him in spite of emotions you might wish he didn't have. Too often, one spouse shuts down the feelings of the other. Six ways to shut down emotional togetherness follow:

• Ignore: "I didn't notice you were feeling that."

• Deny: "You don't feel that."

- Moralize: "You shouldn't feel that."
- Belittle: "How stupid, immature, or selfish to feel that."
- Manipulate: "If you really loved me, you wouldn't feel that."
- Attack: "I am so mad that I want to hurt you."

Any of these six will hurt your emotional togetherness and maybe even destroy it. If you are serious about a great relationship, you must respect your spouse's feelings even if they don't make sense to you or make you feel comfortable. (In fact, it is even more important to respect the other person in these instances.)

So what's the bottom line?

Respect each other's emotions and the two of you grow closer.

Disrespect emotions and you get distance—sometimes a whole lot more distance than you ever expected.

Emotional Management

Every marriage is a potential emotional minefield. On the surface all is calm and peaceful, but just beneath the surface lies danger. Negative or painful events in your history plant landmines. Your unsuspecting partner strolls across your life and innocently takes a wrong step.

Kaboom! Suddenly everything blows up. Without warning your spouse is shocked and scared and wounded.

"Where did that come from?"

"What did I do wrong?"

"Why was I hurt?"

"How can I protect myself so I don't get hurt again?"

Your spouse looks at you, and the love has been replaced by fear. You are no longer safe to be with. You are dangerous and your spouse cautiously moves into a defensive posture and avoids getting too close for fear of triggering another landmine.

The challenge of every couple is to learn how to manage emotions. There are three ways—bury the mines deeper, simply let them explode, or defuse them.

Bury them.

Suppressing your emotions is dangerous. Many people figure that if you bury those unwanted emotions deep enough, you can forget them and they will just fade away.

No such luck.

Buried emotions don't just fade away. They either work themselves back to the surface where they explode with a double fury or their poison leaks out, seeping through the soil and contaminating all it touches.

Let me switch metaphors for a moment.

Stuffing your emotions is like a sliver driven deep into your finger. If you let it lie, it grows red and infected.

Pressure.

Puss.

Pain.

The longer you leave it, the worse it gets until it threatens the whole body. Emotions have to come out, just like splinters and landmines. Here are some of the potential dangers of buried emotions:

- Depression
- Hypertension
- Stomach problems
- Headaches
- Passive-aggressiveness
- Confusion
- Weight gain or loss
- Nightmares
- Phobias
- Addictive patterns

Let them explode.

Acting out your emotions is often just as dangerous as stuffing. Some carelessly let their emotions blow with the attitude, "This is the way I am," or "I can't help myself," or "If I don't let it out, I'll go crazy."

But by exploding, you risk hurting whoever happens to be close. The flying shrapnel of words can cut anyone within earshot. The blinding flash of raw emotion can send anyone running for cover. The reverberating blast shakes even the strongest from their feet and leaves them with lacerated memories that are slow to heal.

Explosions create both external and internal damage that can take years to fully repair. The fallout can plant mistrust and fear. The debris can close down communication. The lingering effects can hurt those you love the most.

Letting it all explode might feel good, but the negative impact is too great. Besides, it rarely builds emotional togetherness.

Defuse them.

Working through your emotions honestly and humbly leads to understanding. To face your landmines and admit that they are yours takes character. To approach and defuse them takes courage.

But what if your partner rejects you or loses respect for you? What if he or she thinks you have too many buried mines? What if he or she finds the wiring on your mines too complicated?

Many are afraid to defuse because of their spouse's possible response. But if you are honest and humble, your partner will draw closer rather than move away. Talking through your most negative emotions without blaming your spouse or parents or anyone else can create an intimacy that brings two hearts closer than ever. To see one's spouse so vulnerable also challenges the other to be honest and humble about his or her own mines.

Good management involves the willingness to proactively work through the negative emotions. This might not seem natural. But it is healthy and it makes for a rewarding marriage. If you are willing to take the risk and move out of your comfort zone, the payoff is incredible.

Here are a few ways to defuse emotions:

- Pray together.
- Breathe deeply.
- Share what is happening inside you.
- Let go of your self-protection.

- Avoid blame or attacks.
- Talk about what you need.
- Initiate positive physical contact.
- Discuss changes to make things better.
- Thank your spouse for listening and accepting you.
- Do something you both enjoy.

Wrap Up

Most marital failures are the result of a lack of emotional togetherness. If you don't connect at a feeling level, you will struggle as a couple. Yet many of you are emotionally disconnected right now. It might be due to:

- your childhood,
- hurt and fear,
- depression,
- anger,
- low self-esteem,
- poor communication skills,
- lack of healthy role-models,
- your partner,
- your personality,
- or the stress and hectic pace of life.

All of these issues might make a marriage more difficult, but they can be worked through. Whenever both partners are committed and motivated to have a great marriage, it can happen in spite of a hundred difficulties. Everything starts with emotional togetherness.

Closet Projects

1. Identify what emotions you have felt today and what emotions you think your partner has felt today. Talk together and see if you are on the same wavelength.

2. Chart your emotional history and share it with each other. Include:
    - When you felt most frightened
    - When you felt most sad
    - When you felt most guilty
    - When you felt most lonely
    - When you felt most angry

3. Determine which of Gary Chapman's five love languages is your spouse's greatest need. Then during the next week meet that need at least once a day.

4. Next time you have a strong negative emotion, name the feeling and write down what triggered it. Then try to figure out how this might be related to some past event.

5. Sit down as a couple and discuss which of the six killers of emotional togetherness each of you has used in the past month. Agree that any time during the next month either of you uses one of the killers, the offender will pay a dollar to the other's favorite charity.

3

THE KITCHEN
Practical Projects

Every house needs a kitchen.

I've never heard of a house without a kitchen, have you? In our house, the kitchen is strategically located between the family room and the dining room. In many ways this room is the center of our house. Somebody is almost always in the kitchen—looking through the cupboards, checking out the refrigerator, fixing something to eat. Even in the middle of the night I've been known to sneak into the kitchen for a chocolate chip cookie or whatever other goody I can discover. Tami and I make a great couple because I love food and she's a great cook. So I can always find some recently baked treat hidden in our kitchen.

The kitchen is more than a place to store food. It is a room set aside to prepare meals and snacks. Therefore it can get a bit messy with grease and potato peelings, coffee grounds, and spilled milk. It is a room of work and chores. Most kitchens have a stove, oven, refrigerator, sink, dishwasher, and microwave. They also have counters. Tami likes counters because she says she needs plenty of work space. Lots of drawers and cupboards are another necessity—full of pots, pans, knives, measuring cups, cheese shredders, and a hundred other tools which make the jobs easier.

This is a space with the perennial activity of getting ready and cleaning up.

Tami enjoys decorating and fixing up the kitchen. She's painted the walls red and placed displays above the cupboards. Several years ago, she became concerned about the floor, as our once sparkling white linoleum started to turn yellow. Over time, dents and cuts appeared where things had been dropped. Then a seam, which had once been nearly invisible, began to crack and curl. That was the final straw.

"Steve," she said with a serious tone, "we've got to do something about this floor."

A week or two later Tami found a cobblestone tile that she fell in love with. We got a bid on what it would cost to install the tile, and it was beyond what we were willing to pay. So Tami approached me with a fresh idea: "I think we could lay this tile ourselves."

"We've never laid tile," I replied.

"We could learn," she said with a cute, persuasive smile.

The next thing I knew Tami and I were on our knees pulling up linoleum, laying down the tile, and spreading grout. For three full days we worked side by side from 8:00 A.M. to midnight. It was hard and tiring, but incredibly rewarding. It was also fun. By the time we finished the job, we knew we were a pretty good team. And the floor looks absolutely fantastic.

Now every time I walk into our kitchen and look at our beautiful cobblestone tile, I am reminded of the joy of working beside Tami and the unifying power of practical togetherness.

Practical Togetherness

"I love marriage," said Courtney. "It's just all the work that goes into it that wears me out and makes me grumpy. Is there any way you can have the fun and romance without balancing the checkbook, disciplining the kids, and cleaning the toilets?"

I agree with Courtney, but marriage is full of hundreds of these ordinary, tiresome tasks. I don't think anybody loves them, but they have to be done. It's these mundane little tasks that keep life moving forward. It's like filling your car with gas—it takes time and effort, and is frequently inconvenient. Yet if you don't do it, sooner or later your car will end up at the side of the road, while you are walking to the nearest service station. There are some things you just have to do. In fact Albert Schweitzer, the nineteenth-century medical missionary, once said that most of life involves taking out the garbage.

Since marriage is full of these practical everyday chores, it would make a lot of sense to make use of these opportunities for togetherness. One of the warmest memories of my maternal grandparents is watching them work together. After the evening meal Grandma Blanche would wash the dishes and Grandpa Walter would dry them. As they worked side by side in the kitchen, they reviewed their day. At the same time, they modeled for an overactive grade-school boy an example of practical togetherness where a husband and wife tackle the everyday tasks of life as a team.

As I've worked with couples over the past 20 years, I've found that they seem to naturally resist this area of togetherness. All too often we divide tasks into "His" and "Her" categories. He pays the bills and she says nightly prayers with the children. He mows the lawn and she cooks the meals. He transports the children and she plans the budget. Every couple divides the tasks differently, but the problem is that most things are divided.

It doesn't have to be this way!

Working together has a lot of advantages. Try it with the three primary areas of practical togetherness: financial management, parenting responsibilities, and household chores. It's a lot easier than doing it alone, and you might be amazed at how it brings you closer.

Financial Management

"I can't believe it," Jack said in frustration. "You know we need to be careful with our money, but you still go out and buy four new outfits."

"But they were on sale," said Jayden.

"If we don't have the money, we don't have the money. I don't care if it is the greatest sale on earth."

I've heard this sort of argument hundreds of times. Money is one of the areas of practical togetherness that can make or break a marriage. God has a great sense of humor. He likes to bring savers and spenders together, and then watch them work out their differences. For many individuals money is a symbol of deeper emotional needs—such as security, success, freedom, or self-esteem. As the world heavyweight champion of boxing Joe Louis once said, "I don't like money actually, but it quiets my nerves."

Smart couples talk about money. They discuss feelings and expectations about their finances. They are open about where they currently are financially and where they want to be in the future. Couples who set goals and plan together have a better chance of being happy together. A great place to start is to discuss what exactly you would both like to do with your money. Which of the following areas would you most like to spend your money on?

God	Savings
Debt	Dreams
Gifts	Charities
Causes	Investments
Home	Utilities
Necessities	Dates
Vacations	Education
Hobbies	Entertainment
Clothing	Medical Care
Transportation	Retirement

"What happened to your marriage?" I asked Jeff.

"Trina was disappointed that I didn't make more money," he explained. "She came from a wealthy family that had everything, and I just couldn't compete. She was used to spending a lot, and she was driving us broke."

"Did you talk about it?"

"No, we couldn't talk about money. It was too sensitive a subject."

"So who handled the bills?"

"I did," Jeff said. "Trina doesn't even know how to balance a checkbook."

"Did you ever work up a budget?"

"I did, but Trina wasn't interested in those sorts of details. She said the finances were a man's job. I couldn't get her to work with me on anything to do with money."

It was not money that ended this marriage; it was Jeff and Trina's lack of practical togetherness. Smart couples take charge of their finances together. Even if they have separate sources of income, they create a place where they can share a portion of their financial resources. Here they work as a team. The money here is not "his" or "hers"; it is "ours." Both partners take interest and responsibility for their joint assets, even if one of the two is decidedly better with financial matters.

Pay your bills together. If you do this, you both know where you are financially. You will know:

- how much things cost,
- how much debt you have,
- how much savings you have,
- and how much expenses have changed.

This way there are no surprises, and when problems arise, they can be discussed before they build to a crisis. Have one partner look at the bill and the other write the check. Then the next month, the two of you change roles.

Plan your budget together. Most couples don't have a budget, and as a result they spend more than they earn. Sooner or later this will catch up with you, putting pressure on your relationship. Financial experts encourage every couple to track their spending for three months. Be realistic, but commit to spend less than you earn each month. If this is not possible, it's time to downsize your expenses and lifestyle. Both of you need to agree with your budget, because if one feels forced to conform, they will not be motivated to cooperate. So once you have accepted a workable budget, develop a strategy to live within its parameters.

Agree to major expenses and changes to the budget together. As members of a team you don't make decisions that impact the budget without both of you being in agreement. Early in our marriage, Tami and I each made a list of things we wished to purchase for our home. Our two lists looked decidedly different. She thought we needed furniture and kitchen items, while I thought we needed a CD player and yard equipment. Together we sat down and determined an order of priority. We affirmed each other's needs, and we worked out when to get each need met in a way that seemed equally fair. Never make a major purchase without your spouse's approval. This is not an issue of getting permission; it's an issue of showing respect and building trust.

Discuss the four special baskets together. After the major expenses are paid, talk about four more areas in which to place your money. Each of these is very important. To ignore them is to diminish your marriage and your togetherness. I call them the four special baskets.

- The Giving Basket: Giving to God, those in need, and various special causes can enrich your marriage.
- The Retirement Basket: Setting aside money for the future can help both of you get the most enjoyment from your golden years.
- The Security Basket: Saving a portion of your income for emergencies or unexpected situations makes good sense. Hope for the best, but prepare for the worst.
- The Dream Basket: Using money for short-term and long-term dreams can add excitement and anticipation to any marriage.

Manage your finances together. This involves talking through every issue that comes up, while realizing that each of you may value and spend money differently. Respect each other, but also admit that one of you might be a better money manager than the other. You may wish to defer to that person, but that should not be allowed to sabotage your togetherness. Some experts say that as many as 80 percent of all divorces are the result of financial difficulties. Therefore manage your finances together or they will mismanage you and then drive you apart. Here are a few financial principles to get you started.

- Talk about your finances regularly.

- Give to God off the top.
- Make a budget.
- Avoid new credit card debt.
- Pay off current credit card debt as soon as possible.
- Have two months of living expenses in savings.
- Plan for your future.

Once a reporter asked John D. Rockefeller, one of the richest men in the world, "How much money do you need to make you happy?"

Mr. Rockefeller stopped and pondered the question. After a few moments, he looked the reporter in the eye and said, "Just a little more."

We live in a world that has become so materialistic and greedy. We are drawn to that which is newer and bigger and supposedly better. Money is not bad, but the apostle Paul warns that "the love of money is a root of all kinds of evil" (1 Timothy 6:10a). This is the challenge of every marriage: to learn how to be content regardless of your financial situation. As an old saying goes, "Money cannot bring happiness—but it certainly puts our creditors in a better frame of mind."

Finances are important, but it is dangerous to make them too important. I have found that many of the best things in life are free—a sunset, children's laughter, a compliment, a cool drink of water on a hot day, peace of mind, good friends, and being loved. Yet we still dream of things and cling to things. I have discovered two basic rules about the stuff we collect:

- The Law of Diminishing Satisfaction: The longer you have something, the less it satisfies.
- The Law of Increasing Dissatisfaction: The longer you have something, the more you long for something more or different.

Finances need to be kept in proper perspective. If you ignore them, you can get into trouble. If you battle over them, you may create distance or distrust in your marriage. Yet if you work together, you will draw closer in this area and so many others. So here are 10 principles that keep finances in proper perspective for Tami and me.

1. Realize that money can't make you happy.

2. Live for what really matters.

3. Know that riches will pass away.

4. Be content with what you have.

5. Put people above money.

6. Share what you have with the ones you love.

7. Invest in the right places.

8. Keep character above acquiring.

9. Don't cling to what you have.

10. Give generously to things that will last beyond your lifetime.

Parenting Responsibilities

Children are a gift from God. They can be delightful and enrich your marriage so much, but there are also those times when they drive you crazy. Life was simpler before children. There was time to relax, pursue hobbies, spend time with friends, and develop togetherness. With children life seems so full and your time doesn't belong to just the two of you anymore. Parenting is often a 24-hour-a-day responsibility. The changing lifestyle accompanying children forces the two of you to be more determined and creative in building togetherness. There is also the added opportunity of a new arena for practical togetherness.

Too often the task of parenting is done individually rather than as a couple. Individual time with your children can be special, but there also needs to be family time. The security, growth, and bonding of a healthy family require a husband and wife who intentionally work together toward a set of common goals. A strong family is one of the most important legacies any couple can leave. So set your goals and work as a team to develop a great family. Some of these goals are:

- Togetherness. Enjoy spending time together.
- Respect. Respect one another's thoughts, feelings, boundaries, and possessions.
- Acceptance, appreciation, and affirmation. Encourage and build one another up.

- Love. Care about one another and communicate your love.
- Rules and responsibilities. Follow agreed-upon rules and share family responsibilities.
- Communication. Talk to one another about what is on your hearts and minds.
- Fun and laughter. Relax and have good times together.
- Honesty. Be honest and truthful with one another.
- Traditions. Set routines, patterns, and traditions that bring you closer.
- Priorities. Live in a way that demonstrates your priorities of faith, family, and friends.

There are at least five major parenting areas in which the two of you can show your practical togetherness.

Know your children.

Every week parents will bring their kids to me with a common complaint: "Something is wrong with my child, but I don't know what."

I sit down with the child for half an hour and then meet with the parents.

"How did it go?" they ask.

"Great!" is my usual reply. Then I go on to tell them all that I learned from their child.

"How did you learn so much in so little time?" they ask.

The answer is easy!

I enter their world and pay attention.

I watch their facial expressions, their movements, their body language.

I listen to their words, their emotions, their strengths and weaknesses, their hurts and hopes.

Knowing your children takes time and effort, but it is worth it. Whatever you learn, be sure to share with each other. It will strengthen your relationship as a couple and your role as a parent. Some of the questions I frequently ask are:

- What is your favorite . . .
    food?

television show?

time of the year?

subject at school?

- Who are your best friends? Why?
- What do you like best about yourself?
- If you could go anywhere in the world, where would you like to go?
- What is your least favorite . . .

chore?

habit?

fear?

place to go?

- What can we do to be better parents?

Love your children.

Every child needs to be loved. Tell them how much you love them. Compliment them and encourage them. They need to hear your words to build them up, because there is so much in life that can tear them down. Too often I hear from adults that their greatest disappointment about their childhood is that they weren't told by their parents that they were loved. Parents hold more influence than anything else in the healthy development of children. A child might know he or she is loved but still needs to hear it regularly.

Children also need to be shown they are loved. If they do not feel loved, they might withdraw inside themselves and find it difficult to give love. This can leave scars that last the rest of their lives. So hold them close. Play with them. Do special things for them. Take them somewhere fun. Surprise them with something they like. There are hundreds of ways to love your children, and here are a few simple ideas.

1. Hug every morning. 2. Go to zoos, parades, and amusement parks. 3. Hang their art and awards on the refrigerator. 4. Create family traditions. 5. Be patient. 6. Apologize when grumpy. 7. Go camping. 8. Play tic-tac-toe and hide-and-seek. 9. Always

carry Band-Aids and gumdrops. 10. Know their strengths.
11. Compliment them. 12. Encourage them. 13. Appreciate
them. 14. Eat meals together. 15. Slow down. 16. Respect their
privacy. 17. Listen. 18. Don't discipline in anger. 19. Be consistent. 20. Say "I love you" frequently. 21. Let them be silly.
22. Accept imperfections. 23. Reward good behavior. 24. Explain
the rules clearly. 25. Laugh often. 26. Go to their favorite
restaurant. 27. Invite their friends over. 28. Buy ice-cream cones.
29. Go on vacations. 30. Know when to be gentle and when to
be firm. 31. Make birthdays unforgettable. 32. Teach responsibility and respect. 33. Choose your battles. 34. Don't embarrass
them. 35. Help with schoolwork. 36. Try to understand their
world. 37. Build memories. 38. Keep promises. 39. Say "no"
when needed. 40. Don't yell. 41. Give gifts. 42. Model virtues.
43. Pray with them. 44. Pray for them. 45. Talk with their
teachers. 46. Tell them you're proud of them. 47. Reach out.
48. Count stars together. 49. Talk every bedtime. 50. Wrap up
with a blessing.

Teach your children.

In the book of Proverbs it says, "Train a child in the way he should go,
and when he is old he will not turn from it" (Proverbs 22:6). There are so
many things children need to know, and it is your responsibility to teach
them. The home should be a primary place for learning, but too often
parents let school, television, books, friends, and other organizations take
over their job. These things are not necessarily bad, but they need to be
carefully monitored.

Ron and Beth thought long about what life-skills they wished to teach
their three girls. Together they developed a list of basic information and
at what age they wanted to focus on it.

When the girls were . . .

8 years old, they studied sexuality.

9 years old, they did the dishes.

10 years old, they vacuumed the entire house.

11 years old, they cleaned the bathrooms.

12 years old, they mowed the yard.

13 years old, they planned the meals.

14 years old, they prepared three meals per week.

15 years old, they planned social events.

16 years old, they paid the bills.

Ron and Beth worked together with a basic plan. Then together they taught these life-skills. Now they have three very responsible college students. Their home training has paid off, and any young man who marries these girls will be extremely lucky.

As parents you teach whether you realize it or not. Your children are constantly watching everything you do. Unfortunately they are quicker to pick up your bad habits than all your good traits. One slip of the tongue, where you say that one word you have never said before, and your child is suddenly all ears. For the next week, your child is repeating that one word over and over again, reminding you of your poor example. Don't give up. Just remember that anything you say or do in private could easily be repeated in public. Also realize that along with everything else you are teaching, two of the most important things are how to be a good husband or wife and how to be a good parent.

Then there is the area of virtue. When I was in college, one of my psychology professors was an outspoken atheist. One day in class she mentioned that she was taking her children to Sunday school the next weekend.

In curiosity I raised my hand and asked, "Why would an atheist take her children to Sunday school?"

"Because I'm a good parent," she replied. "There is no place in our culture, outside the home, where virtues are consistently taught except in churches. Therefore, I make sure my children are in church every Sunday."

If an atheist psychology professor recognizes the importance of teaching virtue, then so should the rest of us. Churches are great places to learn virtue, but I believe this is only effective if it reinforces what's already being taught in the home. Here are some of the virtues I want to teach my children.

- Honesty
- Courage
- Kindness
- Patience
- Faith
- Hard Work
- Purity

- Respect
- Self-discipline
- Compassion
- Humility
- Fairness
- Obedience
- Responsibility

Discipline your children.

As parents you have a responsibility to set rules that teach, protect, and guide your children. Without discipline, your children run the risk of growing up to be spoiled, irresponsible, and possibly even delinquent adults. Discipline brings children from immaturity to maturity. It helps them avoid the foolishness, dangers, and various other pitfalls of life. It teaches them that there are rules to be obeyed, no matter how old they are, and that there are consequences to be paid for disobeying these rules.

Parents who love their children will discipline them. Every individual has a slightly different perspective on discipline; much of this is based upon how they were disciplined as a child. This area can be highly emotional and therefore it is very important that each couple work together. If a child senses differences in discipline styles, he or she will quickly set you up into good guy vs. bad guy roles, doing everything possible to manipulate you against each other. Therefore work together and establish rules of discipline as a team, before you communicate them to your children. Support each other in front of your kids, even if you disagree. When differences of opinion arise, resolve them in private. Your children need to see a united front, especially in this area.

Every couple has their own unique form of parenting, but researchers have divided these approaches into three basic styles.

1. The Marshmallow Style. This is where there are few rules, and those set are often vague and unclear. The discipline has inconsistent follow-through. Children are given a lot of space and little supervision. They believe they can manipulate their way around the rules and talk their parents out of any consequence.

2. The Military Style. This is the opposite extreme of the Marshmallow Style. There are many strict rules that are difficult to understand and/or obey. The discipline is often harsh and might be done in anger. Children frequently become fearful of their parents and might even believe they will get into trouble no matter what they do.

3. The Managed Style. This style draws from the strengths of the other two types, and it has been proven to be the most effective. There are clear rules with calm, consistent consequences. Children know what to expect and that their parents discipline because they love them.

Discuss the managed style together and then figure out how you can implement it as a team. Here are 10 points that will help the two of you be successful in this area.

1. Set clear, age-appropriate rules.

2. Explain the rules and why you have set them.

3. Describe the consequences of breaking the rules.

4. If your child is older, he or she might participate in setting these consequences.

5. Have your child repeat back to you the rules and consequences.

6. When your child breaks a rule, firmly without anger remind him or her of the rule and the consequences. Then follow through with the discipline.

7. If you are angry, don't discipline until you have calmed down.

8. When finished with the discipline, reassure your child that you believe in him or her and that you are sure he or she will make a better choice next time.

9. Tell your children you love them and give them a hug. If a child is not ready to accept one, don't force it.

10. Move on with life without embarrassing children by bringing up their offenses again.

Protect your children.

The world can be harsh at times. It can be full of danger, temptation, immorality, and stupidity. As caring parents you need to warn and educate your children without creating unwarranted anxiety or fearfulness. On September 11, 2001, terrorists hijacked commercial airplanes and struck fear into the American people by crashing into the World Trade Center and the Pentagon. That afternoon my two sons went into our backyard and dug a bunker deep into the clay soil so if planes struck our home we would have a place of protection.

Several evenings later as I was passing eight-year-old Dusty's bedroom, I heard muffled sobbing.

Stepping into his room and sitting on the bed beside him, I asked, "Dusty, what's wrong?"

"The planes are going to come and bomb our house," he said between his heavy sobs.

I put my arm around him while he asked me questions and I answered the best I could. After we had talked and prayed, I asked if he felt any safer. He gave me a nervous smile and said, "I guess so, but could I have one more hug?"

We hugged and I think we both felt better. One of our many jobs as parents is to make our home a safe haven and do all we can to protect our children.

Twenty-five years after leaving home, my three brothers and I are currently spending time with my parents on the beaches of Mazatlan. As an extended family we all get together about once a month. My parents will say, "Once a parent, always a parent—no matter how old your children are." Together they parented us, and at times they still feel like they need to parent us.

Someone once said that the best gifts you can give your children are deep roots and strong wings. These are two invaluable gifts, but I believe the very best gift you can give them is the example of a great marriage. As your children grow up watching the two of you work together, it sets a model which will help them be more successful in marriage. As they watch the two of you grow older hand in hand, it imprints in them a legacy which will not be soon forgotten. So give them the gift of your very best and it will return to you in great abundance.

Parenting as a team, regardless of the temperament, need, or ages of your children, will build a practical togetherness that will make the world jealous.

Household Chores

I hate making the bed.

Tami and I have a queen-sized bed and when I try making it by myself, I have a horrendous time. On one side I have the blanket hanging too far over, so I go to the other side and I either pull it too far or not enough. Then I have to go back to the original side and try to get it right.

But if Tami and I make our bed together, we can do it in a fraction of the time it takes me alone. We also get a chance to talk and encourage each other in the process.

We live in an independent culture where we each want to do things our own way. We naturally seem to divide household chores into a "his list" and "her list." Rarely do we have an "our list," and if we do, it is significantly shorter than the other two. By dividing up so much of what we do, we miss a great opportunity to connect and share a load between two sets of shoulders. By doing chores together they go faster and are often a lot easier. Besides that, it can allow for some great conversation.

There is power in doing things together. So clean the house together. Do your yard together. Paint your family room together. Wash your car together. The payoff makes it all worth it.

Though practical togetherness is the goal, I realize that it is not always as ideal in reality as in theory. When Tami and I try to cook a meal together, it is not always a positive experience. We each approach this task very differently. Tami doesn't use recipes; she throws the ingredients together and then tosses the pans and dishes into the sink. When the meal is cooked it tastes great, but the kitchen looks like a disaster. I carefully measure out each ingredient and follow the recipe to the detail. I clean the pans and dishes as I go along. When the meal is done it doesn't taste as good as Tami's meal, but the kitchen looks cleaner than when I began. Early in our marriage we learned that cooking together was not a good thing for us. Yet I know many couples who have found that cooking together is a wonderful experience.

One of the reasons household chores often become a point of frustration or conflict is that you enter marriage with certain expectations. Leslie and Ricardo loved vegetable gardens. In Leslie's family her father meticulously tended a garden that produced everything from corn and tomatoes to cucumbers and carrots. In Ricardo's family his mother kept the garden. When the two got married they each expected the other to create a garden that would be the envy of the neighborhood, yet neither had any desire or ability to do it themselves. After three years of tension over this area they both decided to share in the responsibility and were surprised to find that they each had a knack for gardening.

Many household chores seem small, but when you start adding them together they take a lot of time and energy. Establishing who does what around the house will save you both frustration and misunderstanding. Some of these tasks might belong to "her" because of time, interest, or skill, while others might belong to "him" for similar reasons. All the same, try to do as many of these side by side as possible. Here are some of the most common household chores.

1. Caring for cars. 2. Cleaning bathrooms. 3. Decorating.
4. Doing dishes. 5. Doing laundry. 6. Dusting. 7. Entertaining.
8. Grocery shopping. 9. Handling correspondence. 10. Ironing clothes. 11. Keeping the house clean. 12. Maintaining the yard.

13. Making repairs. 14. Packing for vacations. 15. Planning meals. 16. Planning vacations. 17. Preparing meals. 18. Purchasing gifts. 19. Recycling. 20. Running errands. 21. Scheduling events. 22. Scrubbing floors. 23. Taking out the garbage. 24. Vacuuming. 25. Winterizing the home.

When you do these tasks separately, make sure you don't take your spouse for granted. Express appreciation, especially if it is a chore that is difficult, time consuming, or something they don't enjoy. When your partner does any household chore, no matter how small, it makes your life easier. It is an act of love and commitment. Recognize it as such and communicate how much you appreciate their work and willingness to do these chores.

"I don't know why I even try," said Sherry. "I slave all day at an office, and then I come home to cook and clean. I wouldn't mind doing this, except Thomas doesn't even notice what I do. I don't even mind that he doesn't help. I just wish that he'd notice."

When I explained to Thomas what his wife needed, he laughed. "Housework is a woman's job. I shouldn't have to help her or thank her. That's just the way it is."

Six months later, Sherry moved out of her home with Thomas. "It's a lot easier to clean up after one, than two," she said. "If he doesn't love me enough to appreciate what I do for him, I guess we don't have much of a relationship."

After two weeks of living alone and doing all the household chores by himself, Thomas learned his lesson. He sent a beautiful bouquet of flowers and a long note thanking her for all she did around the house that made it into a home.

Now they do the chores together and he never misses an opportunity to show his appreciation. So follow Thomas's great example. Recognize your spouse's effort and compliment his or her work. You might even do something special for your spouse or, at least, go into great detail with thanks and praise.

Wrap Up

Some couples take the practical tasks of life very seriously; they work hard and pride themselves on how efficient they are. Other couples do all they can to put off these chores and responsibilities as long as possible. Then there are couples where one person takes these things seriously, and the other is more relaxed about them. Whichever type of couple you are, togetherness in these normal, everyday tasks makes a big difference. This area cannot be easily ignored. Bills must be paid, children must be fed, and laundry must be done. Other areas of togetherness can be ignored for short periods, and a couple can make up for the loss. But with practical togetherness, the tasks accumulate and don't go away. As they build, so can the frustration. But if you regularly do what must be done as a team, life goes so much more smoothly.

When you decide to divide the practical tasks, be careful to do this in a way that's as fair as possible. If both partners have full-time jobs, the division should be adjusted appropriately. But remember that not all chores are equal.

Some are easy, some hard.

Some only take minutes, some take hours.

Some are done but once a year, some are repeated daily or weekly.

For those tasks that are divided, trade off periodically. If she vacuums and he folds the laundry one month, have him vacuum and her fold the next. In that way you both learn what is required for each task, and therefore you develop a greater appreciation of what your spouse does.

Though division of tasks is sometimes necessary, still take every opportunity possible to do the practical aspects of life side by side. Do the dishes together. Make your budget together. Work in the yard together. Discipline your children together. Do as much as you can together, and while you do your tasks, talk and listen, play and plan, smile, and enjoy your time in each other's company. By doing this you not only accomplish your tasks, but you draw closer together and strengthen your marriage.

What a deal!

Kitchen Projects

1. Sit down together and review your current financial situation. If you do not have a budget, make one together. Then figure out what you need to do to live within it.

2. Go out to your favorite restaurant and discuss the Four Special Baskets with each other. Listen closely to the needs, concerns, and desires of your financial partner.

3. What general goals do the two of you have for your family? Together set at least five goals, print them onto a nice poster, frame it, and present it to your children.

4. Look at the list of 25 common household chores. Mark which ones you do, which ones your spouse does, and which ones you do together. Surprise your partner by coming alongside and making more of the "alone" tasks into "together" tasks.

5. This week go out of your way to recognize what your spouse does. Compliment and thank him or her, and then do something special to show how much you appreciate all your spouse does.

THE DINING ROOM
Social Projects

Before we built our house, we had the dining room table. This isn't just any ordinary, run-of-the-mill table. It is an incredible table made from large, solid oak planks. It is 12 feet long and was built about 1880. We liked this table so much that we built our dining room around it. In fact, it fills the entire room. As you walk into our house, stand in our entryway, and look to your right—there it is: our dining room and our oak table.

Sooner or later most guests end up in the dining room. It's a warm and cozy room—a nice place to linger. As a family, we might eat in the kitchen or play games in the family room or visit on the patio. But when we have friends or guests over, we are drawn to the dining room. We gather around our big table and eat or play games or just visit. More often than not we do all three. Nearly every week we have somebody over to sit around our table; sometimes for special occasions, sometimes just to get together. One of our favorite times of the year is New Year's Eve, when we invite three or four couples over and spend the whole evening eating, playing games, and visiting. Then at midnight we go out on the front porch to cheer and light off fireworks. It's a great time to connect with our friends.

Tami loves to have people over   the more often, the merrier. I enjoy people, but I also enjoy my private time. However, Tami has taught me to be more social and we have developed a large group of wonderful friends. Now I am just as likely as Tami to be the one who invites people to come over and sit around our dining room table. Our social togetherness has grown with each year of marriage. Maybe this is because Tami is such a great hostess and she almost always bakes something delicious when people come over—cookies, brownies, pies, cakes, or one of a dozen other confections. Or maybe it's because we've learned how important people can be to a good marriage. Whatever the reason, few people would argue the point that healthy relationships can help a couple enjoy the good times and survive the difficult times.

So grab your spouse's hand, invite another couple over, and sit down at your dining room table. Eat. Play. Visit. It doesn't have to be a special occasion. It just has to happen. Positive couples not only enrich your life, they strengthen your marriage.

Social Togetherness

Eric and Courtney both grew up in Portland, Oregon. They had strong family support and plenty of good friends. They were involved in a small group at their church and went out to the movies once a month with a bunch of neighbors.

Life was good, but then Eric's work transferred him to the East Coast. Saying good-bye to friends and family was the hardest thing Courtney had ever done. As the years passed I had lost contact with Eric and Courtney. Until several months ago, that is.

"Is this Dr. Steve?" asked a familiar voice on the phone.

"Yes, how may I help you?"

"This is Eric and I'm alone in a hotel room holding a loaded gun to my head," said a shaky voice. "Courtney and I divorced six months ago. I'm so lonely and it hurts so bad. You were the only person I could think of to call."

"What happened to get things to where they are today?" I asked.

Eric sighed. "When we moved east, it was very hard on Courtney. She missed Portland and we couldn't find any real friends. We visited several churches, but none of them were a good fit. We even tried to get together with our neighbors, but they already had their friends and they were too busy for us. Courtney finally found some friends at work, several ladies who had just gone through divorces. They didn't believe the same way we did, but I didn't want to rock the boat. I was glad Courtney had found some friends and started smiling again.

"But Courtney began pulling away from me. After work, she'd go out with her friends to a local lounge and wouldn't come home until ten or eleven. I told her I wished we could spend more time together. She got mad and accused me of trying to control her life. So I backed off and started working more and more overtime. Soon our relationship started falling apart."

"But you and Courtney had such a great marriage while you were here in Portland," I said.

"We had friends and family and people who cared about our marriage in Portland. We had a positive support system," said Eric. "I'm convinced that if we hadn't moved we'd still be married today."

"How can you be so certain?"

"A couple has to have support," said Eric as the emotions overtook him. "A couple just has to have support."

Eric was right.

Every couple needs other people who are willing to stand beside them. Social togetherness involves connecting with people who can enrich and strengthen your marriage. The difficulty is, we live in a culture where we are so independent. We tend to isolate ourselves. When things are great, we don't think we need anyone. When things are not so great, we don't want to bother others.

Eric survived his season of despair, and through it all he learned how important people can be. He returned to Portland where he was greeted by family and friends. Now he is trying to rebuild his life.

If you want a healthy marriage, you can't ignore the social side. You must consider at least four aspects of social togetherness.

Quality Friendships

Hopefully your spouse is also your friend. In fact some of the best marriages develop out of friendship. Yet you also need friendships outside of marriage. Kahlil Gibran, the philosopher, wrote, "Let there be spaces in your togetherness." These spaces can be filled by healthy outside friendships. Your spouse cannot possibly meet all your social and interactive needs; to expect this places an unfair burden on the relationship.

There is something to keep in mind about this, however: Friends should draw you closer to your spouse; they should never pull you away from him or her. Therefore let me give you some precautions in terms of outside friends. Beware of friends who:
- are negative about marriage,
- don't respect your spouse,
- think they are better than your spouse,
- don't like spending time with your spouse,
- have a different value system,
- are too demanding on your time,
- take much more than they give,
- constantly are in crisis,
- are of the opposite sex.

The above friendships might be innocent, but they could undermine your marriage or at least create an unnecessary level of stress. They might be very nice people, but they run the risk of threatening your spouse or marriage. And remember, your spouse must take priority over any outside friendship, no matter how long you have known them, how close you are to them, or how much you enjoy your time with them.

Healthy, nonthreatening friends are an asset to a good marriage. My wife, Tami, gets together with a group of women she has known since grade school. Once a month she also meets with eight ladies from our old neighborhood. It seems like every day Tami is spending time with a friend or two. If she doesn't meet them face-to-face, she's on the phone with them. These friends encourage and energize Tami. They make her life richer and our marriage smoother.

One day Tami warned me that several of her closest friends were out of town. "Are you ready?" she asked.

"Ready for what?"

"I'll need you to talk with me a lot more than normal," she said. "I'll need more time, attention, and encouragement."

I was glad she warned me. Without her friends, her expectations of me increased. Friends provide a place to vent frustrations, check out perceptions, talk about things our partner has no interest in, and participate in activities our spouse doesn't care about.

I'm supportive of Tami getting together with healthy friends and she also encourages me to hang out with the guys. This strengthens our relationship and causes us to appreciate each other more. Our togetherness is a priority, but this need not minimize the value of good friends. After time with our friends, both of us reconnect refreshed and with a stronger sense of togetherness. Friends are important because they:

- laugh with us,
- cry with us,
- build memories with us,
- stand beside us,
- confront us,
- believe the best in us,
- help us grow,
- keep us from temptation,
- and enrich our lives.

Individual friends are great, but shared friends are invaluable. They become your marital support system.

Support System

Every marriage needs other couples with whom you can relax. Other married couples can show you what is normal, healthy, and positive in a relationship. They can give you a safe context to explore what is working and not working in your marriage.

Tami and I have a number of couples we get together with regularly. We meet with Dan and Sue, Todd and Monica, and Dan and Shanni to talk about parenting. We go to the movies with Roy and Joyce. We play cards with Gary and Debra. We get together with about five couples for a small group at church every other Sunday night. Once a month we join three other couples to go out to dinner together. (It's been several months since we've done anything with Monte and Tammy; we keep thinking that we need to set up something soon.)

These couples are our support system and vice versa. Each of these couples is unique, but there are important similarities. In a positive support system we:

- respect each other,
- respect marriage,
- have a common faith,
- have common values,
- can be honest,
- can be ourselves,
- and have at least some mutual interests.

With such supportive couples you can learn from their successes and failures while following their strengths and avoiding their weaknesses. In so doing you mature as a couple, a spouse, and a person. By learning from each other you gain a healthy and solid perspective in many areas. Support systems model:

- honesty,
- sensitivity,
- respect,
- encouragement and empathy,
- communication,
- problem solving,
- togetherness,

- romance,
- commitment.

A good support system keeps you on course. These other couples model how to show love and work through the difficulties that challenge every relationship. They help you make mid-course corrections when you discover that you have somehow veered off the proper vector. Without this sort of support system many couples have strayed into hurt and tragedy. With this support you have a means of protection that you will not regret.

Accountability Groups

Couples can keep each other accountable, but when men meet with men and women meet with women the discussion can cut deeper. When challenged by a spouse or someone of the opposite sex, one tends to get defensive. Yet a friend can say the same thing and you can accept it. You need a small group of your gender to confront, admonish, warn, encourage, and hold you accountable for the things you know you should do or the things you know you should not do.

Guys get together with other guys and ask some tough questions. Here are ten to get started.

1. Have you taken your wife on a date this week?
2. When did you last lose your temper?
3. What has been your greatest struggle this week?
4. What is one thing you wish you hadn't said or done this week?
5. How have you shown your wife that she is special to you recently?
6. What television shows or films have you watched lately?
7. What is the most questionable site you've visited on the Internet?
8. How is your walk with God?
9. Whom have you avoided, neglected, slighted, or offended this week?
10. How would your wife rate your marriage today?

Bonus question: Have you minimized or manipulated any of the above answers?

Now gals, it's your turn. Meet with a few gal friends and ask a few of your own tough questions. Here are 10 approved by Tami.

1. What is the worst attitude you've had this week?
2. How many times have you grumbled or gossiped this week?
3. Is there anybody to whom you need to apologize?
4. How many minutes have you spent praying for your husband in the last week?
5. What are you currently holding against your husband and why?
6. What do you need to do to prepare yourself to forgive him?
7. What have you done lately to encourage and build up your husband?
8. What have you read or watched on television this week?
9. Have you sought attention or approval from places and in ways that aren't the best?
10. Is there any unconfessed sin in your life this week?

Bonus question: Which of your above answers have been less than fully honest?

Don't feel limited by these questions. Make up your own. Create new ones and get rid of those that don't apply to you. The important thing is that you look deep and are open to growth. An accountability group that meets on a regular basis and is not afraid to be honest—sometimes brutally honest—can do wonders to the growth of your marriage.

Mentor Couples

Everybody needs a mentor couple. This is a couple you can respect and who shows a level of maturity that makes them good guides. They aren't perfect, but they know how to walk together through difficult passages. This couple can teach you through words and example how to succeed. They know what holds a marriage together and what can tear it apart. When I look for a good mentor couple, I look for the following qualities.

• They have been married ten years or more.
• They are committed to each other.

- They have good conflict resolution skills.
- They can communicate what they know.
- They desire to grow spiritually and are active in pursuing that growth.

Throughout Scripture we have examples of older, more mature men coming alongside younger men. Moses mentored Joshua, Eli taught Samuel, Elijah was a role model for Elisha, and Paul guided Timothy. We all need help. Likewise it says in Titus 2:4 to have the older women "train the younger women to love their husbands and children."

It only makes sense to connect those who have more experience and wisdom with those who are just starting out or with those who have run into difficulties. In fact I would encourage the use of a mentor couple during engagement, during the first year of marriage, during major communication and/or conflict difficulties, during periods of emotional disconnect, and during any time you wish to grow closer together.

Mike McManus, the founder of Marriage Savers, says that "the greatest untapped resource to save marriages is couples with solid marriages to share their life experience with others." In fact Mike and his wife, Harriet, have personally mentored over 50 couples. "Several evenings out of our life are a small thing, but it can be life-changing for a couple," says Harriet. "It is also one of the few ministries husbands and wives can do together."

Mentoring saves marriages. If you are a young and struggling couple, find a mentor couple. Look for a pair with experience, integrity, availability, and a good relationship. If you are mature and have a solid marriage, consider being a mentor couple. You don't need to have it all together; you just need to be honest, committed, and willing to share. Things that you have learned over the years that seem so obvious to you might not be so obvious to another. Older generations have much to offer. They can and should train younger generations. Through doing this, wisdom, knowledge, and stability are passed on. In so doing, marriages are strengthened, supported, and hopefully saved.

Yet there are unique challenges that make some marriages more difficult than most. When couples hit these challenges, many choose to give up and proceed immediately to divorce.

This need not be.

There is hope.

Many couples have experienced the same challenges as you and have survived. Some of the greatest challenges are:

- unfaithfulness,
- death of a child,
- infertility,
- blended families,
- acting-out children,
- addictions,
- deep depression,
- financial devastation,
- overwhelming health problems,
- and explosive anger.

All of these—and more—can be worked through. It is not easy. It does not happen quickly. But your marriage can survive. However, there are several things you must do. You both must be willing to take action.

- Deal with the issues of change.
- Take responsibility for your part of the difficulty and show genuine repentance.
- Let go of the past and move forward to make a new life together.
- Strengthen your reliance on God.
- Make a deeper, less selfish commitment to each other.
- Try to find a mentor couple who has successfully worked through a challenge similar to the one you've experienced.

But what do you do with a mentor couple? You get together with them regularly and share your toughest struggles. You honestly disclose your frustrations and fights. Don't pretend you have it all together. Faking it will just keep you stuck where you are. I know it's awkward sharing personal stuff with others, but that's how growth happens. Once you've let it all out, listen. Let others give you insight from their years of experience.

You will have a delightful time.

You will learn things you never thought of.

You will strengthen your marriage.

So get a mentor couple or be a mentor couple.

Wrap Up

Years ago John Donne wrote a famous poem with the line "No man is an island." He was right! We all need each other. Adam needed Eve, Moses needed Aaron, David needed his mighty men, and Nehemiah needed hardworking citizens to rebuild the city wall. We all need social interaction, whether we are willing to admit it or not.

"Let us not give up meeting together," says the author of Hebrews (10:25).

Why?

Because gathering together encourages, strengthens, teaches, keeps you on course, and reminds you of what is right.

It has always been interesting to me how many couples socially disconnect prior to divorcing each other. It is as if they know they will be questioned by those who care, perhaps even challenged. So it's easiest just to distance themselves from people and drop out. When Ben's marriage hit difficulties, he stopped talking with his friends. He feared they would not be sympathetic to his actions. He also stopped spending time with his support system. He was concerned they might not agree with him, and might actually side with his wife, Anna. Then he started skipping meetings with his accountability group. He knew they would confront him with his selfishness and anger problem. When Anna suggested they call their mentor couple from church, Ben laughed and stomped out of the house.

"What do they know?" he shouted. "They've never been in my shoes. They wouldn't understand. Besides, it's my life and I don't want anybody to tell me what to do."

Six months later Ben and Anna divorced.

Ben had been like a ship in a terrible storm. Instead of staying in the harbor with the other ships, he cut his moorings and allowed himself to drift out to sea. Without adequate protection, the wind and waves beat upon him until he sank.

Storms will come into your marriage, but don't be as foolish as Ben. Don't cut yourself off from quality friendships, support systems, accountability groups, or mentor couples. These might well be exactly what you need to protect your marriage.

Without them, sooner or later the wind and waves will do their damage. Your once-treasured ship will sink and all you once had will lie beyond your grasp in the murky waters of regret.

Dining Room Projects

1. Evaluate your closest friends, determining whether they are healthy or unhealthy friends.

2. Encourage your spouse to get together with his or her healthiest friends at least once a month.

3. Invite another couple with common values, whom you both like, over to your house or apartment on a regular basis.

4. Join an accountability group and see if your partner is willing to do the same. If you can't find one, start one. Once you've found your group, ask hard questions and be real.

5. Find a couple in your church or community whom you really respect, and invite them out to dinner with you. If you have been married less than five years or have any unresolved challenges, ask them to be your mentor couple.

6. If you have been married longer than 15 years and have a stable marriage, consider being a mentor couple.

5

THE FAMILY ROOM
Recreational Projects

After a hard day's work, I like to come home and kick off my shoes and sit in the large overstuffed chair in our family room. I put my feet up on the ottoman, turn on the TV, and relax. Tami comes in and sits on my lap. This is where we can both relax. We rarely do work in this room. It's a place set aside to laugh, play, have fun, and just hang out.

Tami and I have a cozy family room. It holds a large chair, a comfortable sofa, a CD player, and an armoire with a TV and DVD player hidden inside. Ours is a simple family room, but we enjoy it. I know couples who fill their family rooms with everything from exercise equipment to pinball machines, foosball games to Ping-Pong tables. I even know a couple with a trampoline in their family room. All of these things are great, because they give you a chance to have fun.

Several years ago our kids convinced us to get a GameCube. We hooked it up and now we have weekly video game competitions. We laugh and cheer each other on, but I usually lose. Yet we have a great time. In the hall beside the family room we have our game closet. During rainy days in winter we light the fire, Tami makes hot chocolate, and we pull out our favorite games—Monopoly, Life, Sorry, Boggle, Clue, Scrabble, or Battleship. We sit cross-legged on the floor and the hours disappear as we laugh and joke and try our best to win. As you can probably tell, Tami and I both have a competitive side. We both like to win, but we never forget that the purpose of our games is to enjoy our time together.

The television can be dangerous or an enormous waste of time. Yet it doesn't have to be either. In too many homes the television is the primary piece of furniture in the family room. We hide our television behind the doors of an armoire, so we have to be intentional about watching it. Each year Tami and I choose one show which will be "our show." We snuggle up on the sofa and watch "our show" together—discussing the characters, anticipating what's going to happen, and reminiscing about past episodes. During many weeks, we also might have a DVD night where we find some new or classic movie and have an "in-house date." We get a bowl of popcorn and I put my arm around my beautiful wife, and we watch our movie until the late hours of the night.

The family room is a wonderful room. It's full of fun, excitement, and activity. It's one of my favorite rooms. It's a place where positive memories are built. It's a place where recreational togetherness flourishes.

Recreational Togetherness

How did the two of you meet?

Where was your first date?

What sort of things did you like to do when you were getting to know each other?

When did you realize this was the person for you?

I love to ask couples these types of questions. When they answer, their eyes twinkle and a smile raises the corners of their mouths. These early memories are usually some of the most treasured. They are filled with joy and laughter, fun and relaxation, romantic dates and shared adventures. It's what I call recreational togetherness.

It's interesting to me that recreational togetherness draws two strangers into marriage. But then as the stress and responsibilities of life build, recreation is one of the first things pushed from the schedule. There just doesn't seem to be the time, money, or energy to do what you once did. So the things that helped bring you together are now ignored. No wonder couple after couple come into my office saying they've lost the magic, the passion, and maybe even the love they once had.

"You haven't lost it," I usually say with a smile. "You just aren't taking care of it. Go back to the things you did when you first met and the spark will return."

Try it and you'll be amazed! The five aspects of recreational togetherness include sports, relaxation, fun and laughter, weekly dates, and getaways. Try one or two and soon you'll be convinced. Before you know it you'll be doing all five. And I promise that you'll never regret it.

Sports

Debbie and Jim played tennis together four to five times a week before they married. They were both competitive and excellent at the game. They were also equally matched, with neither of them the consistent winner. Six years into the marriage they sat in my office arguing over who watched the most television. "How many times have you played tennis since your wedding?" I asked.

The couple stopped their argument and stared at me.

I stared back, waiting for a reply.

"More than 10 and less than 30," said Jim.

"That's too bad."

"Why is that?" asked Debbie.

"Because if you put all the energy you devote to fighting into a game of tennis, I bet it would be an incredible game."

Two weeks later Jim thanked me for helping them rediscover their sport. "Once we stepped back on the court we had such a great time that we forgot about our petty disagreements."

Getting involved in a sport together can reenergize your relationship. Whether it is something strenuous like soccer or something more relaxed like walking, there is a sport for every couple. Not only is it good for your marriage, it is healthy for you as an individual.

When you are physically active you:
- feel better,
- handle stress better,
- grow stronger,
- sleep deeper,
- act kinder,
- reduce anger,
- draw others closer,
- and live longer.

Every individual has favorite sports. Tami likes bowling, horseback riding, golf, and soccer. I enjoy basketball, bike riding, swimming, and waterskiing. We both encourage each other in our individual sports. It's fun watching Tami on a soccer field giving it her all. And she is supportive when I limp home after an aggressive game of basketball. Yet the most fun comes when I join her for bowling or horseback riding, or she joins me on bikes or water skis.

We have a great time with sports. When we were first dating we tried windsurfing, but my balance is not as good as Tami's. I spent most of the time in the water, while she skimmed across the surface laughing at my frequent mishaps. We love to hike, and in the Pacific Northwest we are never far from a place of beauty. So we hike the beach, to the top of Multnomah Falls, or through the sagebrush of the high desert. Another activity we have shared is snorkeling. Together we marveled at the underwater colors off St. Thomas, were stung by tiny jellyfish off Puerto Vallarta, and fed the fish frozen peas in Hanama Bay in Oahu.

Tami and I have canoed, ice skated, played volleyball, and skied (both downhill and cross-country). But one of my favorite memories is catching the waves on a boogie board in Mexico. The water was warm, the sky was blue. It was a perfect day. We swam out into the Pacific Ocean about two hundred feet and tried to catch the biggest waves just before they'd crash over us. It was great fun, but it was hard for us to catch the same wave. Suddenly a huge wave moved toward us. We steadied our boards and prepared to push up at just the right moment. Just before the wave broke I pushed up and caught it. I was at the perfect point, riding the edge of a giant wave, when I looked over and saw Tami just three feet away riding the same wave with the same thrill. The moment was priceless and unforgettable. We both smiled and held on to our boards for dear life until the sea dropped us not so gently onto the sand. But for that short ride, our recreational togetherness was flawless.

There are other sports we'd like to do together. We'd like to golf or snowshoe. Yet, there are certain sports I have no desire to do with Tami or anybody else. Hang gliding and hunting are two sports that don't fit my personality. The idea of dangling high above the ground from some flimsy contraption or pointing a gun at some harmless animal doesn't create much excitement. Other than these two, I'm open to trying most sports at least once. Here are 50 athletic activities you might want to try together.

1. Aerobics 2. Archery 3. Baseball or Softball 4. Basketball 5. Bicycling 6. Billiards 7. Bowling 8. Canoeing and Kayaking 9. Dancing 10. Fencing 11. Fishing 12. Frisbee 13. Football 14. Golf 15. Gymnastics 16. Handball 17. Hang Gliding 18. Hiking 19. Hockey 20. Horseback Riding 21. Horseshoes 22. Hunting 23. Ice Skating 24. Jogging or Running 25. Martial Arts 26. Motorcycle Riding 27. Ping-Pong 28. Racquetball 29. Rock Climbing 30. Rollerblading 31. Sailing 32. Scuba Diving 33. Skateboarding 34. Skiing (cross-country, downhill) 35. Sky Diving 36. Sledding 37. Snowboarding 38. Snowshoeing 39. Snowmobiling 40. Soccer 41. Snorkeling 42. Surfing 43. Swimming 44. Tennis 45. Volleyball 46. Walking 47. Water Polo 48. Waterskiing 49. Weightlifting 50. Windsurfing

Relaxation

Sports are fun, but sometimes you want to sit back and catch your breath. I love activity, but at times it is nice to simply relax. On those days you'd rather watch sports than play them. When we were first married Tami knew I liked to play basketball, but she wasn't ready to step onto the court to play a sometimes brutal game with me and my brothers. Yet she wanted some recreational togetherness, so she started watching the Portland Trail-blazers with me. She learned the rules of basketball and discussed the players and cheered for our home team. Together we'd relax and have a great time. But after two or three seasons Tami became a bigger fan than me. Now every time our Portland team is televised she is watching, and I watch gratefully beside her.

In our hectic, fast-paced, always-on-the-move world we don't relax as often as we should. Even God rested on the seventh day after creating the heavens and earth. When too many people and life pressures crowded in on Jesus, He said to His Disciples, "Come with me by yourselves to a quiet place and get some rest" (Mark 6:31). There are many times I'd like to turn to Tami and say very similar words, "Drop what you're doing and come with me to a quiet place where we can find a little rest and relaxation."

When we are always on the run, it is hard to connect. The faster we run, the more superficial our relationship becomes. To truly connect we must slow down and look at each other. It's hard to see when life is a blur. We also need to take the time to carefully listen to the words, feelings, and concerns of the one we love.

When I am in a hurry, distracted, or not really interested, I might skim a book. This gives me a general sense of the content, but it doesn't give the true heartbeat of the author. Yet if I pick up a book which has been highly recommended by someone I trust, I will read more slowly and intentionally. I will take my time, savoring each sentence and contemplating each page. By the time I have finished, I feel like I know the author. In our time with our spouses we frequently skim the surface, missing much of the joy and meaning that could be ours. I beg you to slow down and savor your relationship. Let me suggest some ways to slow down.

1. Don't wear a watch.
2. Do only one thing at a time.

3. Claim a media fast:
> No TV
> No radio
> No CD or tape player
> No telephone
> No computer or video games

4. Focus on each individual moment.
5. Take a nap, a walk, a bath (or all three).
6. Let the day set its own pace.
7. Savor the little things:
> Look at the details
> Listen to the rhythms
> Touch the textures
> Taste the wonders
> Smell the nuances

8. Recognize the miracle of each other and enjoy every second together.

We all have hobbies. These are the activities that help us relax and bring us joy. They distract us from the stress and worry of everyday life. Most of the time we do our hobbies alone or with a same-sex friend. Yet I'd like to suggest you develop marital hobbies. I know a couple who works together on a crossword puzzle every morning. Another couple plays cribbage each night when the husband returns home from work.

Sharing a hobby brings a couple closer. When Tami and I were dating, we'd play video games together. In the past few years Tami has developed the hobby of gardening. Each spring and summer she is outside tending her flowers. One of my hobbies is reading, and I enjoy spending a peaceful evening absorbed by a well-crafted book. Over the years we have learned to share our hobbies. Together we spend sunny afternoons trimming plants and laid-back evenings turning pages. The great Roman philosopher Cicero wrote that the only two things a person needs are a garden and a library. Tami and I would agree, with one significant addition:

We believe you also need someone with whom to share these two special places. If you have a hobby, kick off your shoes and share it together. If you don't have one, look at the following list and find one to try.

1. Animals 2. Antiquing 3. Art 4. Astronomy 5. Board Games 6. Boating 7. Calligraphy 8. Camping 9. Card Playing 10. Cars 11. Ceramics 12. Coins 13. Collecting 14. Comedy 15. Computers 16. Cooking 17. Crafts 18. Crossword Puzzles 19. Decorating/Design 20. Drawing 21. Entertaining/Hospitality 22. Floral Arranging 23. Gardening/Landscaping 24. Geology/Rock Hunting 25. Glassblowing 26. Jigsaw puzzles 27. Journaling/Writing 28. Model Trains 29. Movies 30. Music 31. Nature 32. Origami 33. Painting 34. Remote control airplanes 35. Photography 36. Pottery 37. Quilting 38. Reading 39. Rocketry 40. Sculpting 41. Sewing 42. Shopping 43. Stained glass 44. Stitchery/knitting 45. Television 46. Theater 47. Video games 48. Volunteering 49. Weaving 50. Woodworking/woodcarving

Fun and Laughter

"Enjoy life with your wife . . ." (Ecclesiastes 9:9a) said King Solomon, one of the wisest men this world has ever known. Yet most couples work too hard to really enjoy their life together. They feel that if they aren't doing something useful, they are wasting time. Sigmund Freud, father of psychoanalysis, wrote that the healthiest people know how to work hard and play hard. Playfulness is a forgotten aspect of love. Couples who know how to play and have fun together develop a bonding that can carry them through the most difficult of times.

Yesterday afternoon the kids in the neighborhood had a giant water fight. There were water balloons and large water guns. Hoses were pulled into the street and buckets were filled to overflowing. The kids chased each other and drenched each other, all the while laughing and cheering and having a great time. As I watched, I was struck by how naturally kids know how to play and have fun. As adults we seem to have lost our playfulness. Even fun has to be planned and scheduled and budgeted. Yet for most kids, fun is just around the corner. They can find it anytime and anywhere: cardboard boxes, bubbles, mud puddles, dirt, sidewalk chalk, or a piece of string. As adults there is so much we can learn from children.

"Fun is serious business," say Dave and Claudia Arp, best-selling authors on marriage. Some of my favorite times with Tami have been having "serious" fun together. We built sand castles at Cannon Beach and gingerbread houses in our kitchen. We have played cards by firelight and volleyball in the bright summer sun. We have had fun in a thousand ways, for fun isn't just what you do. It's a frame of mind and with an attitude of playfulness. You can have fun wherever and whenever.

A part of fun and playfulness is laughter. In the classic movie *Mary Poppins,* there's a wonderful song entitled "I Love to Laugh." Just listening to this song makes me want to chuckle. More of us should learn to laugh, for laughter brings a couple closer and can cut through the tensions which develop in any relationship.

Last winter Tami and I took our three kids to Disney World. As we were flying home, the plane ran a sitcom on the video screen. This show somehow struck my funny bone and within minutes I was laughing until tears streamed down my face. The more I tried to control myself, the harder I laughed. Looking around to see if others were laughing too, I was relieved to see that they were. But they weren't watching the video screen. They were watching me.

I love to laugh, especially with Tami. Look for something that touches your funny bone and laugh together. Ask each other what it is that gets the two of you to laugh; what is your funniest TV show, joke, movie, person, memory, activity, or story?

In the book of Galatians there is a list of nine positive characteristics called the fruit of the Spirit. The second in this list, right after love, is the quality of joy. We all need more joy, and with joy come fun and laughter. I was talking to a young couple the other day and they agreed that they need more fun. "But where do we start?" they asked. Here are 50 ideas that point you in the right direction.

1. Bake cookies together. 2. Blindfold your spouse and take them somewhere special. 3. Blow bubbles. 4. Collect rocks, shells, etc. 5. Count your blessings. 6. Create balloon animals. 7. Dance in your living room. 8. Draw pictures and color them. 9. Dress up in your nicest clothing and go nowhere. 10. Finger paint. 11. Have a water fight. 12. Have an egg toss. 13. Hold a kissing clinic. 14. Imitate the funniest people you've ever met. 15. Laugh until your sides hurt. 16. Learn a new card game together. 17. Listen to your favorite CD. 18. Make funny faces. 19. Make love by candlelight. 20. Make the tallest ice cream sundae you can. 21. Plant a garden. 22. Play charades. 23. Play croquet or bad-minton. 24. Play hide-and-seek. 25. Put a love note where your spouse can find it. 26. Put makeup on each other. 27. Put together a scrapbook showing the high points of your marriage. 28. Read Dr. Seuss books to each other. 29. Reenact your wed-ding day. 30. Rent your funniest video. 31. Ride a carousel or Ferris wheel. 32. Roast marshmallows. 33. Send flowers for no reason. 34. Share scary stories. 35. Shoot off fireworks. 36. Sing in the shower. 37. Sleep in the backyard. 38. Snuggle together on the sofa and watch a good sitcom. 39. T.P. a good friend's house. 40. Take a bubble bath together. 41. Take pictures of each other. 42. Talk about your favorite memories. 43. Talk in rhyme for one hour. 44. Tell jokes. 45. Throw a party. 46. Tickle each other. 47. Walk in the moonlight. 48. Watch cartoons. 49. Work in the yard together. 50. Write a romantic poem together.

Weekly Dates

Kim and Greg didn't know how to have fun. Kim was a stay-at-home mom with three small children, and Greg was a highly-stressed corporate accountant. By the time they interacted at the end of the day, they were both exhausted. They were committed to each other, and they knew they loved each other, but everyday survival had crowded out the positive feelings that had once made them feel so close.

"When is the last time you had fun together?" I asked.

"It's been a long time," said Greg.

"When is the last time the two of you have gone on a date?"

"Let's see," said Kim. "Our oldest child is seven and the last date I remember was just before she was born."

"So your last date was seven years ago?"

"Yes," they both nodded.

"No wonder the two of you are struggling."

The following week Kim and Greg went out on a date. They laughed and had fun and enjoyed getting away without their kids. When I saw them next they said they were going on a date every week.

"It has revolutionized our marriage," said Greg. "I don't know why we ever stopped dating."

"I don't know why we ever waited so long to start again," said Kim.

There are a lot of excuses for not doing what is healthy. Here are a few I've heard over the years.

- Too busy.
- Not enough money.
- Can't agree on what to do.
- Too tired.
- Too frustrated with each other.
- Nothing sounds like any fun.
- In a rut.
- Can't find child care.
- Afraid to be alone with each other.
- Don't know how.

Dating sometimes takes planning, but it is worth the effort. The two excuses I most often hear for not dating are: we are too busy, and we don't have the money. We are all too busy, but you just have to schedule it and make it happen. If you wait until it's simple or convenient, you might have to wait a long time. If money is a problem, there are a lot of activities that cost little or no money. I know a couple who go walking for their dates. Another couple go to a local coffee shop or bookstore for their time together. If you are creative, it's amazing what you can find to do. Remember it's not where you go that's most important, it's that you spend quality time together.

When you have small children at home, dating can sometimes be a challenge. Yet this is a phase of marriage when dating is the most important. No matter how much you love your children, you need a break from them every once in a while. Connect with other couples with whom you can trade off babysitting. One couple I know watches a neighbor's kids each Thursday night, while the neighbor watches their kids every Friday night. Trading children can save you money and give you a much-needed break.

Here are some basic rules to help you make your marital dating successful.

- Make dating a top priority.
- Ask your spouse out formally.
- Set up a date night on a regular basis.
- Trade off on who plans the dates. (She plans one, he plans one, then it's her turn again.)
- Be positive if your partner chooses a place that isn't your favorite. (Remember it's who you're with, not what you do, that's important.)
- Be creative and don't get into the rut of doing the same old thing.
- Make sure you spend some time during the date talking and listening. But don't talk about finances, children, or problems on a date.
- Do something romantic.
- Hold hands.
- Have fun.

Dating takes creativity. Doing the same thing over and over can diminish the excitement of any dating activity. Dates can come in many shapes and sizes. A date might be squeezed into a full day. It might be an out-on-the-town date or a stay-at-home date. Some dates are romantic and some are practical. Some might be private, with just the two of you, while others include another couple or even a crowd of friends. Be creative and try a lot of different types. Here are a few ideas.

1. Airport 2. Amusement park 3. Bike riding 4. Breakfast date 5. Bubble bath and chocolate 6. Candlelight dinner 7. Music store 8. Coffeeshop & bookstore 9. Concerts & musical events 10. Count the stars 11. Dancing 12. Dessert & great conversation 13. Explore a nearby town 14. Favorite restaurant 15. Feed the ducks 16. Find someplace you've never been 17. Fly kites 18. Give each other 20 compliments 19. Give each other full body massages 20. Go for a drive 21. Go on a treasure hunt 22. Go to a party 23. Help someone else 24. Home Depot date 25. Japanese garden 26. Look at houses 27. Look at photographs together 28. Make a gourmet dinner together 29. Make out 30. Movies 31. Museum 32. Pajama date 33. People watching 34. Picnics 35. Planetarium 36. Plan your next vacation 37. Play games 38. Plays 39. Read a book together 40. Relive your first date 41. Reminiscing 42. Snuggle up by a crackling fire 43. Sports events 44. Stroll around your neighborhood 45. Surprise your spouse 46. Take a class together 47. Take-out dinner and a romantic video 48. Walk through a park 49. Watch a sunset (or maybe even a sunrise) 50. Zoo

Getaways

Every couple needs a getaway at least once a year. Some years it might just be for a long weekend, but perhaps you can escape for at least a week every couple years. These getaways are very important for connecting. There are three stages to these vacations:

Stage 1: Planning. This can be a lot of fun. Spending time gathering brochures, reading maps, looking through books, and checking out

Websites can increase the anticipation of your trip. Talking and dreaming about your escape makes it seem so much more special before you ever even leave your home. I know a couple who has been planning a trip to Australia for nearly 20 years. Whenever you talk to them about vacations they will sooner or later ask if you've been to Australia. And if you have, they will ask a hundred more questions. Each year they save a little more money for their dream getaway and each year they discover something new about "the land down under." They are having a wonderful time. The wife once told me that even if their getaway never happens, it would all be worthwhile because the planning is the very best part.

Stage 2: Experiencing. Tami and I love getaways. As I write these words we are at a beach cabin on the Oregon coast with a few good friends. When we are away from the schedule, responsibilities, children, and telephone, we find it's easier to relax and connect. We share all sorts of new and exciting experiences. The uniqueness of this adventure draws the two of us closer. When you escape, try new things and fill your time with as much fun as you can, for these are special moments that you will never forget.

Stage 3: Remembering. Planning and experiencing getaways are great, but remembering them is my favorite time. I love to reminisce about the horse and buggy ride through Central Park, the sun filtering through the ancient trees of the redwood forest, and the sparkling blue ocean as we landed at sunset in Bermuda. I have thousands of these memories and each time I recall them, I recapture a magic moment that Tami and I shared together.

Memories are a powerful link between any couple, and getaways make sure these memories are positive. As we race through the frustrations and franticness of everyday life, little reminders can take us back to those wonderful memories. Whenever Tami and I see a horse, she leans toward me and whispers, "His name is Rambo." Suddenly our minds are transported back to a great vacation in Puerto Vallarta.

Tami enjoys horseback riding, while I know very little about this activity. But at a ranch outside of Puerto Vallarta, they insisted Tami ride "Strawberry" and I ride "Rambo." The names of these two horses perfectly fit their personalities. Strawberry was gentle and slow and compliant. Rambo was wild and fast and independent. Rambo galloped everywhere at full speed and I learned quickly to hold on to the horn of the saddle with both hands and pray that I wouldn't die. Apparently I wasn't the most graceful looking cowboy on the ranch, for when I glanced over at Tami she was laughing so hard she almost fell off her horse. Now she periodically reminds me of Rambo and my remarkable equestrian style.

You all have special memories of getaways. Treasure these times and don't forget them. In fact, every couple should have a memory box where they can periodically pull out something that will take them back to that special time and place. Positive memories soften past hurts and losses. They allow you to relive the joys you've shared together. They also deepen your appreciation of each other and strengthen your commitment to a good marriage.

Once a year plan a vacation or getaway together. Make a list of all the places near and far that you would like to visit. Then figure out how and when you could turn a few of these into reality. Here is a list of trips you might consider.

1. Alaska 2. Alps 3. Australia 4. Branson, Missouri 5. Camping 6. Canada 7. Caribbean Islands 8. Castles of Great Britain 9. China 10. Civil War battlefields 11. Deserts 12. Disneyland/ Disney World 13. Exploring caves 14. Florida Everglades 15. Grand Canyon 16. Germany 17. Great Barrier Reef 18. Greek Isles 19. Hawaii 20. Holy Land 21. Hong Kong 22. India 23. Ireland 24. Italy 25. Japan 26. Local Bed and Breakfasts 27. Lakes and rivers 28. London 29. Mesa Verde National Park 30. Mexico 31. Mountain climbing 32. Museums of Europe 33. New England in the fall 34. New York City 35. Niagara Falls 36. Paris 37. Pyramids of

Egypt 38. Redwood Forest 39. Russia 40. Safari in Africa 41. San
Francisco 42. Scandinavia 43. Ship cruises 44. Skiing in the
Rockies 45. South America 46. Spain 47. Texas 48. Visiting the
beach 49. Washington, D.C. 50. Yellowstone National Park

Wrap Up

Recreational togetherness is what brought you together, and it can keep
you together. Life is busy and there is so much to do, but in the midst
of this hectic pace it is important to find the time to relax and have fun.
King Solomon wrote, "There is a time for everything and a season for
every activity under heaven . . . a time to weep and a time to laugh, a
time to mourn and a time to dance . . ." (Ecclesiastes 3:1, 4). Don't let
the weeping and mourning crowd out the laughing and dancing.

Recreational togetherness might seem like an irrelevant, superficial,
and/or optional aspect of marriage, but that is far from the truth. This
chapter has touched on five aspects to recreation: Sports, Relaxation,
Fun and Laughter, Weekly Dates, and Getaways. Each of these are
important. Adding positives to a marriage increases its strength, satisfaction, and longevity. With these five additions you are guaranteed to
enrich your marriage and have a lot of fun in the process.

Family Room Projects

1. Talk about what sort of sports each of you has done in
   the past and which you would like to do together in the
   future.

2. Go through the "50 Hobbies" listed earlier in this chapter
   and choose three or four of them you will do together.

3. Collect your five funniest jokes and tell them to each other
   just before you go to bed.

4. Set aside two hours to do something you both consider frivolous and fun.

5. Write down the qualities and activities you think would make the most romantic date, then make it a reality.

6. Choose a getaway place your spouse would like to go, then start planning a vacation there for just the two of you.

6

THE STUDY
Intellectual Projects

Books have always intrigued me. Even as a small child I was fascinated by all the wonders that filled the pages of a simple book. Every volume I picked up was full of ideas I'd never thought of, people I'd never met, and places I'd never visited. Books have stretched, shaped, and inspired me in ways I never thought possible.

In our house we have a study. It has a lot of shelves and a lot of books. It also has a table, a chair, and a computer. The computer has replaced many libraries, for it can give you access to millions of books and many more ideas. We like our computer, but we also like our books. Together they dwell side by side in our study, friendly competitors in their bid to provide us intellectual stimulation.

Our study is a quiet retreat from the hectic pace of life. It's a magical place that can take us anywhere. It's a room of learning and discovery. I want a couch in our study so Tami and I can sit together, read, and share our thoughts. We are both drawn to different reading material, but we enjoy talking to each other about what we've just read. Tami likes inspirational novels, gardening books, and home decorating magazines. I like literature, history, and Christian thought. I love listening to her tell about what she's just read; her enthusiasm and excitement draws me closer to her.

Every couple needs a study of some sort. My parents had a long, thin study with one wall packed with books. Both of my grandparents had bookshelves as a part of their family room. My Uncle Harry and Aunt Sofie had a beautiful study overlooking Puget Sound in Washington; it was full of windows, maps and *National Geographic* magazines. I know a lady whose study is comprised simply of a rocking chair and a short shelf of books in the corner of her bedroom.

I guess a study is more a frame of mind and an attitude toward life, than a separate room in your house. Study is a noun, but it can also be a verb. It represents ideas, growth, learning, exploration, and discussion. A couple committed to this sort of intellectual togetherness will be a couple who doesn't grow bored or disconnected. So enjoy your study and, if you don't have one, make one.

Intellectual Togetherness

"We're doomed!" said the woman in the well-worn jeans and flannel shirt.

I kept quiet and let her talk.

"We aren't stupid," Cassie said with a hint of defensiveness. "But if you were to describe Gabe and me, intellectual isn't the first word that would come to your mind."

Intellectual togetherness is not about how smart both of you are. It is about sharing your thoughts, ideas, opinions, and beliefs. It's about the excitement of discovery in an amazing world and how enjoyable it is doing it as a couple.

There are three parts to this discovery: recognizing your strengths, stretching your minds, and discussing your thoughts.

Recognize Your Strengths

God has given you and your spouse remarkable abilities. As King David said, we are "fearfully and wonderfully made" (Psalm 139:14). You and your partner were specially crafted by God. Each of you were given strengths. The challenge is to recognize both your strengths and theirs.

My research has identified 10 intellectual strengths. Most people are brilliant and outstanding in at least one or two of these areas. At the same time everybody has several areas in which they are slightly backward!

Don't focus on your or your partner's weaknesses. Instead, focus on your strengths. There are at least six ways to do this:

- acknowledge abilities,
- compliment abilities,
- encourage abilities,
- respect abilities,
- learn from abilities,
- appreciate abilities.

As I describe 10 intellectual abilities, highlight those that belong to you and those that belong to your spouse.

1. Verbal intelligence. This is the ability to put your thoughts into words. Writers, poets, and public speakers can express themselves in language, finding the right word for the right situation. Others find that sharing their thoughts and feelings in language is nothing short of frustrating. They search and search for the right words and never seem to find them.

2. Mathematical intelligence. People with this ability love numbers. They do not need calculators to add, subtract, multiply, or even divide. Calculations come naturally to them. They snicker at those of us who have math phobias or who struggle in this area.

3. Visual intelligence. This ability involves seeing size, shapes, angles, distance, and perspective. It also involves seeing the interaction between objects. If you have good visual intelligence you can even discern subtle hues of color and shadow. Artists, architects, and carpenters have visual intelligence.

4. Musical intelligence. I envy those with the ability to sing and play instruments. Some read music and others can play by ear. My parents insisted that I take four years of piano lessons in hopes that I might develop some musical ability, but it didn't work. Meanwhile, my brother Dale, who never had any piano lessons, can sit at the piano and reproduce almost anything he has ever heard. He has musical intelligence.

5. *Mechanical intelligence.* This is the ability to use one's hands to fix things. Mechanics, plumbers, electricians, and repairmen usually have this ability. Traditionally it's a man's field, but if something breaks in our home, I rarely know what to do. My grandmother once told me you only need one tool to fix things—a hammer. If something doesn't work, you start tapping it until it does.

6. *Logical intelligence.* Problem solving, trouble shooting, and thinking in a sequential manner are all a part of this ability. Corporate executives, business administrators, and anybody involved with management have logical intelligence. These people think clearly from point A to point B to point C. All is in order and well structured. Organization is their middle name. They keep the world running smoothly, but they also drive those of us who are less logical a little crazy.

7. *Physical intelligence.* Dancers, athletes, and actors all have this ability. They are aware of their bodies. They can control and coordinate their muscles with strength, grace, and expression. These people enjoy physical activities and participating in sports. They are naturals at basketball, tennis, or golf. The rest of us sit on the sidelines and covet just an ounce of their abilities.

8. *Personal intelligence.* The person with this ability is in touch with feelings, needs, and motives. In an attempt to better understand themselves, they study psychology. His or her world is inward and at times introspective as he or she ponders personal identity and the reasons for it. They are fascinated by thoughts and emotions, likes and dislikes, beliefs and dreams.

9. *Social intelligence.* This is the ability to bring people together and help them feel relaxed. They can make a group laugh or organize them into action. People naturally gravitate to those blessed with social intelligence. This person might be an up-front leader, but he or she might just as likely be a behind-the-scenes type person.

10. Spiritual intelligence. Some people have an awareness of God and the intangible forces of the universe. They possess a special sense of good and evil. Those with spiritual intelligence have an extra measure of faith and can see beyond what is visible. This ability is possible for more than saints and mystics; it is also possible for everyday people such as you and me.

Once you have recognized your partner's intellectual strengths, it is important to respect and honor him or her in that area. Tami is much better than I in mechanical intelligence, so I regularly defer to her when the garbage disposal or the dishwasher breaks. Yet, I am better than Tami in areas of verbal intelligence, so whenever I speak at a conference she encourages and compliments me.

So learn from your spouse. Let him or her teach you. As you do so, you are preparing for the next part of intellectual togetherness.

Stretch Your Minds

Years ago I read that the average person stops thinking deeply or creatively when classroom education (whether eighth grade or Ph.D.) is completed. I hope this is not true! Formal education is only the springboard for a lifetime of discovery. If you aren't stretching your minds together, your marriage is missing something big.

Without intellectual togetherness there are three specific types of danger:

1. The Rutted Marriage. This is where neither partner stretches his or her mind. The relationship is boring and stagnant. It has lost its life and energy.

2. The Lopsided Marriage. This is where only one partner stretches his or her mind. Here one person is growing and discovering, while the other is not. In time this couple will become more and more distant. If the non-growing person does not wake up, the spouse will become bored and dissatisfied, and will be tempted to look for someone more intellectually stimulating.

3. The Parallel Marriage. This is where both partners stretch separately, but don't share their discoveries with each other. These
partners are on different tracks and have lost their sense of
togetherness. They need to go back and reconnect emotionally.
Once that is done, the sharing of their thoughts, ideas, opinions,
and beliefs will be much easier.

A healthy marriage is where both partners stretch their minds
together. Let me share some ways in which this might happen.

Read together.

"If you read any book that impacts you, I will read it also." That was the
commitment Sheldon and Davy Vanauken had to intellectual togetherness. They earnestly desired to stay mentally close, and the sharing of
books was their symbol of this togetherness.

I mentioned this story to Shirley, who was feeling disconnected from
her husband. And then I asked her, "What has Bob been reading lately?"

"Don't go there," was her immediate reply. "The only thing Bob ever
reads is westerns, and I hate westerns."

"Have you ever read a western?" I asked.

"No, but . . ."

"How important is your marriage?"

"I love Bob, but . . ."

"If you want intellectual togetherness, read what he is reading."

Shirley sighed.

That night she asked Bob the title of his favorite western novel. Then
she asked if she could borrow it.

"Why?" he asked.

"To read."

A smile crossed Bob's face.

During the next year Shirley read three westerns and had several great
discussions about them with Bob.

Not only does reading the same books bring togetherness, but reading to each other can draw you close. I know a young couple who has read

all of C. S. Lewis's *The Chronicles of Narnia* to each other. Another couple is reading a book on parenting. Recently Tami and I began a devotional for couples entitled *Night Light* by James and Shirley Dobson. One night Tami reads to me and the next night I read to her. Afterward we discuss what was just read. The time together is great.

So stop for a moment and think about what you might read as a couple. Maybe it's a book or a devotional, a magazine, or even the daily newspaper. Now that you have an idea, pray about it. Ask God for the perfect time and words to present the idea to your spouse. Here are 30 books that might be fun to read together.

As for Me and My House by Walter Wangerin
At Home in Mitford by Jan Karon
Ben-Hur by Lew Wallace
Emma by Jane Austen
The Five Love Languages by Gary Chapman
The Gift of the Magi by O. Henry
His Needs, Her Needs by Willard F. Harley, Jr.
In His Steps by Charles Sheldon
Jane Eyre by Charlotte Brontë
Love for a Lifetime by James Dobson
Love Life for Every Married Couple by Ed Wheat and Gloria Perkins
The Marriage Masterpiece by Al Janssen
Men Are from Mars, Women Are from Venus by John Gray
The Mystery of Marriage by Mike Mason
The Power of a Praying Wife and *The Power of a Praying Husband*
    by Stormie Omartian
Redeeming Love by Francine Rivers
The Romance Factor by Alan L. McGinnis
Romeo and Juliet by William Shakespeare
Sacred Marriage by Gary Thomas
The Sacred Romance by Brent Curtis and John Eldredge
The Seven Principles for Making Marriage Work by John Gottman

A Severe Mercy by Sheldon Vanauken
Song of Solomon
Sonnets from the Portuguese by Elizabeth Barrett Browning
Stories for the Heart by Alice Gray
Surprised by Joy by C. S. Lewis
Ten Great Dates to Energize Your Marriage by Dave and Claudia Arp
The Testament by John Grisham
To Understand Each Other by Paul Tournier
When Bad Things Happen to Good Marriages by Les and Leslie Parrott

Study together.

Will loved history. He researched and wrote alone as his wife, Ariel, encouraged him along the way. After completing the first few volumes of *The Story of Civilization,* Ariel joined Will as his writing assistant. Side by side they studied, researched, and grew close. As their thoughts and interpretations wove together, Will found that the two had truly become one. The last five volumes of this monumental history have Will and Ariel Durant boldly listed as coauthors.

Stretching your mind involves looking at those subjects of common interest, gathering information, and sharing what you've learned from each other. Studying isn't boring, if it's in an area that fascinates you. Develop a healthy curiosity and have fun.

The Mayan ruins in Central America have always captured my imagination. Wildlife is more interesting to Tami. So when we went to Chitzan Itza in Mexico, we studied both the ruins and the wildlife.

Together we had a blast!

Find your areas of interest and study them together. If you can't agree, then visit each other's areas, inviting one another to join in. Love stretches beyond personal interests. Whatever delights your spouse soon becomes a delight to you. Life is no longer divided into "you" and "me." A new entity takes shape that gently melds two unique personalities into a "we." The "you" and "me" still exist, but both willingly, excitedly, lovingly submit to "we." Now we both are fascinated by ancient Mayan pyramids and the graceful beauty of a soaring hawk.

Let me provide a few ideas that might intrigue you:
- Science
- History
- Politics
- Philosophy
- Literature
- Current events
- Economics
- Geography
- Psychology
- Theology

Circle your favorites and stretch your mind.

Learn together.

Life is an incredible classroom if your eyes, ears, and mind are open. Every day I learn something new, and it is exciting to share this discovery with Tami. A couple that is constantly learning will never become tired of or bored with each other.

I am amazed at how many opportunities we have to learn something new. Each day there are new experiences, new data, new connections, new mysteries, and new challenges. I know a couple who has been taking Spanish courses so they can communicate with the Latino families in their community. Another couple goes to a cooking class, and they have transformed their kitchen into an exciting place of togetherness. A third couple recently attended a workshop on Swedish massage, and now they ease the stress from each other's shoulders whenever the tension builds.

These couples are having a great time building intellectual togetherness. Look for classes, lectures, seminars, or workshops in areas of mutual interest. Then go out together and learn everything you can. If you get stuck, here are some types of classes that you can attend together:

- Acting
- Aerobics
- Archeology
- Art
- Astronomy
- Bible study
- Computer
- Cooking
- Foreign languages
- Gardening
- Genealogy
- Geology
- Hiking
- Investing
- Marriage improvement
- Music
- Nutrition
- Parenting
- Photography
- Reading group
- Swimming
- Travel
- Woodworking
- Writing

Explore together.

What would you most like to explore as a couple?

- a cave
- a museum
- a ghost town
- a bookstore
- a deserted island
- a garden
- a mountain
- a city
- a jungle
- a desert

The possibilities are only as limited as your imagination.

Tami and I love adventures. On our honeymoon we explored the back roads of Maui. Since then we have explored the streets of our own hometown, along with those of New York City, Washington, D.C., Seattle, Orlando, Puerto Vallarta, San Francisco, and San Diego. It seems that around every corner there is another adventure.

We also love to drive the open road, and in our 22 years of marriage we have explored 21 states. One summer we journeyed through Yellowstone National Park and the Rocky Mountains. Five years later we drove to Mesa Verde, the Painted Desert, and the Grand Canyon.

You can explore in your own backyard or a different country. You can walk together through a park, along a beach, or in a mountain meadow. You can drive across your state or across your country. You can fly anywhere. But wherever you explore together, go side by side and stretch your mind to all the amazing places in God's creation.

Discuss Your Thoughts

After reading a book, watching a movie, or hearing a sermon, then talk about it. Share your thoughts and opinions. Show your spouse how and what you think. Sure your spouse might disagree or see it differently. But as you discuss your personal perspective, you move closer in intellectual togetherness. Exposing your beliefs encourages growth. In my marriage, discussion frequently stimulates a chain reaction where Tami's idea triggers a new idea in me, which leads her to another idea. This is the beauty of true interchange—she gives to me and I give to her. Together we have intellectually stretched beyond what either would or could have alone.

Evaluate.

Everything you experience, you evaluate. You either like it or dislike it. Did it challenge you or leave you bored? I encourage you to experience life together and then evaluate it together. Whether it's a concert, Sunday school class, or a television show, it provides an opportunity for evaluation. So don't just experience an event; evaluate it as a couple. Ask each other:

What was its message?

Was it done well?

Was it enjoyable?

Was it thought-provoking?

Was it emotionally powerful?

Was it true?

Was it helpful?

Was it wholesome and moral?

Would you recommend it to a friend?

Did it teach you something new?

Did it draw you closer to each other?

Did it draw you closer to God?

As you evaluate and interact, you will better understand the one you love. This understanding leads to intellectual togetherness, but this does not mean there will always be agreement.

Debate.

There are certain things on which it is important to agree, but much of life is made of opinions, preferences, and interpretations. We all see life from our own unique angle based upon our differing personalities, backgrounds, and experiences. Therefore, much of life is debatable.

In our first year of marriage, Tami and I had a house built for us. This is a great way to discover differences. We debated about design, floor coverings, color schemes, and wallpaper. To debate is healthy. It teaches you the balance of honesty and sensitivity. You don't debate to win, but rather to understand better who your spouse is. Tami's preference in color was different from mine, and she was not easily swayed. We learned how to debate and respect our differences in the process. In the end we learned intellectual togetherness.

There is no need to be threatened by differing perspectives. They are good, healthy, and normal. Exposure to each other's individuality broadens your perspective while deepening your sensitivity. It teaches you much about each other.

Debate is great!

But in marriage it must always be done with virtue. Show your love, patience, honesty, selflessness, and mutual respect. As you disagree and

debate with these principles in mind, you will grow closer as you understand more. Here are a few fun, debatable areas. Which do you think is
best?

Art	or	Science
Lyrics	or	Melody
Books	or	Magazines
Europe	or	Asia
Morning	or	Night
Sight	or	Sound
City	or	Country

Dig.

Good questions are like a sharp shovel. They allow you to dig below the
surface and discover what's buried. If there is a golden coin three feet
underground, and you want that coin, grab a shovel and dig. But if you
don't dig, you'll never get the gold. Likewise, often you don't know because
you haven't asked.

"How do you know so much about my wife after just 45 minutes?"
asked a husband of two years.

"I asked a lot of questions and I listened," was my simple reply.

He shrugged his shoulders in frustration and said, "I wish I knew how
to do that."

If you feel like that, here are a few questions to ask your spouse:

• What have been the high points of your life?
• Who is the most influential person you have known?
• What is the best advice you've ever heard?
• If you won a million dollars, what would you do with it?
• What is your deepest hurt and greatest dream?
• What do you think is the secret to true happiness?

Questions bring you closer. They open your eyes and your heart and
your communication. They take you beyond the superficial and draw you
toward intellectual togetherness.

Wrap Up

Dewitt and Lila Bell Wallace were fascinated with ideas. They were both interested in a wide variety of subjects and they loved discussing these with each other.

In February of 1922, this couple launched a small magazine to promote intellectual togetherness. It consisted of about 30 condensed articles, one for each day of the month, which covered topics from politics to health to real-life drama. It was a magazine that could be read by couples and then discussed together. The articles were short, so they wouldn't take too long to read. They were also varied, so if you weren't interested in today's article, you could wait until the next day and read about something totally different. In the process you would grow closer together.

Over the years their little magazine grew. Now printed in 17 languages, *Reader's Digest* sells over 28 million copies a month and the company grosses some 500 million dollars a year.

I guess intellectual togetherness really pays off.

So go to your local grocery store or bookseller and pick up the latest issue of *Reader's Digest* or any other magazine that holds a mutual interest. Relax with a hot cup of coffee or a cold glass of lemonade and read it to each other.

Stretch your minds.

Discuss your thoughts.

Build your intellectual togetherness.

Study Projects

1. Write down your spouse's top three areas of intelligence. Look for opportunities to encourage him or her in these areas.

2. Find a book, devotional, or magazine that is of mutual interest. Sit close and read it to each other at least three days a week.

3. Some time in the next year, take a class or workshop together.

4. Go exploring within a half-hour drive of where you live. Once there, see how many discoveries you can make together.

5. Snuggle up on your sofa and watch a television show or movie together. When it is finished, evaluate what you saw using the 12 questions presented earlier in this chapter.

6. Write a list of 20 questions about your spouse that will help you get to know him or her better. Place the questions in the glove box of your car. Next time you drive together, have the passenger pull out the list and ask a few of the questions.

7

THE HALLWAY
Conflict Projects

A hallway isn't really a room. Yet most houses have one or more. They are passage-ways from one place to another. They connect various rooms. Without a hallway, a house tends to lose its flow. The house I grew up in had a hallway that connected the family room to the bathroom and bed-rooms. Our current house has a hallway that connects the entryway to the family room, study, and bathroom. Hallways are places of transition, full of comings and goings.

Hallways can be dangerous. When I was seven I broke my toe racing down our hallway. I've also slipped on wet floors, knocked things off the walls, and tripped over stuff stacked in hallways. In fact, I'm frequently telling my youngest son, "Don't put your stuff in the hall." He patiently explains that he either doesn't want it or doesn't know what to do with it, so he sets it in the hall.

One of the difficulties of halls is that they tend to be narrow; our hall-way is three and a half feet wide. Under most situations that is adequate space for two careful people to pass each other without incident. Yet if you're going too fast, not paying attention, or in an unhappy mood, there is the risk of a collision. If I am going one direction down the hall and

Tami is going the other, we need to make sure we maneuver around each other. If I insist upon walking down the center, there will be potential contact or conflict. Now Tami might stop or jump out of my way, but she won't be happy with my lack of consideration or hallway etiquette. Or if I am walking fast and furious down my side of the hall but somehow cross the center line, I might sideswipe her. The comings and goings in any household run the risk of conflict.

Hallways can be difficult, but they are necessary. Hallways teach us to be less selfish and more sensitive. With hallways we learn when to keep quiet, when to shut doors, when to slow down, when to apologize, and when to notice that our partner has their arms full. Yet most important of all, we learn when to hug each other and give those words of encouragement that say, "We can make it through this particular disagreement or challenge." Hallways remind us that conflict is a passageway that gets us to that particular room we want to be in. Conflict togetherness can be a positive place. But first we must learn how to handle it with grace, love, and wisdom.

Conflict Togetherness

It was a cold night. Snow fell and the wind blew. It was the sort of night that calls you to curl up in front of a crackling fire.

Deep in the forest there was a clearing where two porcupines shivered in the cold, one on the east edge and one on the west. As the snow grew deep and the wind took on a sharp bite, the porcupines slowly drew together. The closer to each other they moved, the more heat was conserved and the more protected they were from the wind.

However, there was a problem in getting too close—their quills poked each other. Pain shot through each body and they quickly parted. Escape from the stabbing quills felt so good, but soon the cold pressed in again, and the two found themselves slowly and cautiously moving together. It was comforting to be close until the quills pricked, and the pain once more seemed greater than the cold.

As night progressed, the two porcupines pulled together—then apart, over and over throughout the night.

We are all porcupines and we have all experienced the quills of each other. Sometimes you are the prickly one and at other times your spouse is the prickly one. Unfortunately life rarely goes as smoothly as you wish it would. Putting two imperfect people close together will sooner or later create difficulties and with those difficulties come the quills.

The key for us porcupines is to use our quills in healthy, nonhurtful ways. The porcupine next to us is not our enemy. They might look scary when their quills are out, but our spouse is our friend and ally, our confidant and encourager, our teammate and lover.

How you handle the conflict between the two of you is one of the most important factors determining whether you will have a successful marriage.

Understand the Basics

When you tackle any new subject, you have to start with the basics. Most of our conflicts are somewhat embarrassing. We don't want to air our dirty laundry with others, so we keep quiet about our fights. Yet our silence sends the message that healthy, normal couples don't fight and that all fights must be bad or shameful. This is not the case. Here are three of the basics of conflict.

It is universal.

Every couple fights. This is partially because each person is unique and sees situations differently. I think we should clean the kitchen as we cook. Tami thinks we should clean up after the meal. I think certain colors go together; Tami strongly disagrees. I have certain landscape plans for our yard; Tami has a different plan. These are just a few of our differences; you and your spouse have your own. These differences give life variety and excitement. They also lead to disagreements that turn into conflicts. A conflict is an opportunity to express your perspective and understand your spouse's.

A conflict-free home is unrealistic. Conflict and making peace are hallmarks of true intimacy. Two mature individuals try to live in harmony as a couple, though they realize that differences in personality will naturally lead to some level of conflict. Yet every healthy conflict ends in resolution and reconnection. The resolution might not be what you had hoped for, but only spoiled children insist on always getting their way.

It is normal.
A marriage dispute is not necessarily a sign of trouble. Conflict is natural and inevitable. Any two people who spend much time together are going to have their share of disagreements. However, a conflict is not the same as quarreling. A quarrel is negative, critical, and usually destructive. The book of Proverbs teaches that "a quarrelsome wife is like a constant dripping" (Proverbs 19:13). This is obviously true of a quarrelsome husband, too. Quarrels are exhausting; they wear you down and make you feel a little crazy. Quarrels tend to be circular—they don't seem to go anywhere. Conflicts move toward a conclusion and, if handled maturely, leave a couple better off than when they started. The very worst way to handle conflict is to:

- avoid,
- threaten,
- dig up the past,
- blame,
- belittle,
- explode,
- manipulate,
- refuse to make up,
- or try to win, rather than resolve.

It is an opportunity.
The value of conflict is to resolve difficulties. But in the process a lot more can be accomplished.

A disagreement is an opportunity to be honest about our feelings without being hurtful or abusive. Through a conflict we come to understand our mates better, their likes and dislikes, what is important to them, in what areas they are sensitive, and what they believe. This can be an exciting interaction, for as each of you understands these areas of your lives you will move closer together in your marriage.

Conflict does not need to drive a wedge between you and your spouse; it can actually weld you together through closer understanding. Proverbs says, "As iron sharpens iron, so one man sharpens another" (27:17). If a conflict is approached with a healthy attitude, then both partners are sharpened. Each spouse respects the other when the disagreement is resolved. Both will have grown in their relationship. Yet this only occurs if fights take place in a context of love, with each partner agreeing to fight fair.

Be Prepared for the Top Six

Most couples aren't that creative about their conflicts. They tend to repeat the same old fights until they just about have the lines memorized. Yet there are six areas in which couples most often confine their fighting. In fact, sometime during your marriage, you are bound to have at least one fight in each of the following areas:

Fight factor #1: Money.
Once a month Tom paid the bills and this was the one day Brigit hated most.

"What was this check for?"

"How did this credit card get so high?"

"Why can't you keep on budget?"

With each question Tom got louder and redder and more intense until there was a fight. A key concept for this area is to **manage** your money.

Make a budget and keep it.

Adjust your budget to include money for giving, saving, and investing.

Never use credit that cannot be paid back quickly or on items that cannot be secured.

Agree on all purchases over $50.

Give each other an equal amount of personal money.

Each day thank God for all you have.

Fight factor #2: Relatives and in-laws.

Our parents and relatives are important to us, even if they drive us crazy. Your spouse probably feels the same way about your parents and relatives. Our family of origin is important to all of us. Someone once said that to marry a person is to marry his or her family. Here are a few principles to decrease conflicts over **family.**

Find ways to honor each other's parents.

Always keep your family out of marital conflicts.

Make sure you never put down or attack each other's family.

Include relatives in your holiday plans.

Love the people your spouse loves.

Your spouse should always take priority over relatives and in-laws.

Fight factor #3: Parenting.

Each parent deals with the children in his or her own style. These styles are either an adoption of how you were parented or a reaction against how you were parented. One parent might be stricter, while the other might be more nurturing. One might have high expectations, while the other is more laid back. One might focus on academic performance, while the other emphasizes social etiquette. Don't let your differences detract from the fact that you both love your children. Remember that what is important is that you are both **childwise.**

Consistency is crucial.

Have patience with mistakes and immaturity.

Identify your child's strengths and build on them.

Let them know you love them daily.

Don't yell at or belittle your children.

Watch out for your over-reaction.

Inspire your child to better behavior.

Set reasonable boundaries, and enforce consequences if the boundaries are broken.

Express respect for and togetherness with your spouse, even when you disagree.

Fight factor #4: Sex.

Affection and sexuality are very personal aspects of a marriage. On top of this, men and women often approach these areas very differently. Affection and sexuality are expressions of your love, but they can easily get twisted and contaminated. Your parents' attitudes toward sex, childhood abuse, teenage experiences, physiological drives, emotional security, body image, self-talk, marital expectations, and a host of other factors determine how you approach this area. But in the midst of all this, don't forget that a healthy sexual relationship within the confines of your marriage is critical for your **bonding** together.

Be sensitive to each other's needs and comfort zones.

Organize a romantic setting.

Note that women spell sex: T-A-L-K.

Don't demand sex or manipulate for it.

Initiate a sexual time at least once a week.

Never rush romance.

Give yourself to your spouse with a gentle, gracious, and other-centered attitude.

Fight factor #5: Chores.

"It's just not fair."

"I do 80 percent of what needs to be done at home."

"She just lets the place get out of control."

"Why do I always have to remind him to do what he said he'd do?"

In our hectic, overcommitted, fast-paced world, who does what around the house can become a very heated argument. Certain jobs just have to be done. But whose job is it? Should she be responsible for cooking dinner, cleaning the house, and keeping the family schedule? Does he have to manage the finances, keep up the yard, and take out the garbage? What is really fair?

Regardless of how you distribute these common household chores, don't forget about the importance of **teamwork.**

Talk about expectations.

Each do more than your fair share.

Assign areas of responsibility.

Make sure the kids are involved.

Work together on chores.

Organize "chore times" and "fun times."

Recognize, acknowledge, and appreciate what your spouse does.

Keep open to periodic reevaluation of who does what and making appropriate readjustments.

Fight factor #6: Communication.

This area is key to any healthy marriage. If you can't communicate clearly with your spouse, you will get trapped in an endless cycle of conflict in at least one and maybe all of the above areas. Trouble with communication is the number one difficulty for married couples. If you take this issue seriously, many of the other difficulties in your relationship will get resolved. So memorize the following steps and learn how to truly **communicate.**

Commit yourself to fully listen.

Offer to talk whenever your spouse wishes.

Meet your spouse's needs without complaint.

Mind your manners.

Understand that negative words do great damage.

Never go to bed angry.

Initiate positive conversation.

Compliment daily.

Attend to your spouse's feelings.

Tell your spouse often that he or she is loved.

Express your appreciation for God bringing the two of you together.

Identify the Real Issue

Couples often fight over the silliest things: colors, clothes, directions, memories, television, restaurants, and a host of other issues. By themselves these things might seem trivial, but they are usually symptoms of something deeper. So first define the difficulty and then go beneath the surface.

Not all difficulties are the same, so take the time to determine what kind of conflict you have. There are four types of difficulties.

- A difference. No two people are the same. They are bound to have different opinions and perspectives.
- A problem. This is a difficulty that must be dealt with and has a possible solution.
- A predicament. This is a severe problem that has no easy or satisfactory solution.
- A crisis. This is a very large predicament with an extreme sense of urgency.

Now that you know what you are dealing with, you can move to the next step: Go beneath the surface.

Ask yourself what your underlying need is and what your spouse's need is. Find out what the fight is really about. Don't get distracted by the details. Look to the heart of the matter. What do you want?

- To be right
- To be heard
- To be loved
- To be secure
- To move forward
- To protect yourself
- To protect someone else
- To be respected
- To be understood
- To understand

Once you admit what you really need, you are ready for what may be the most important part of this process.

Take Responsibility

We live in a world of crybabies where taking responsibility is the exception rather than the rule. We love to blame anybody and everybody when we hit a difficulty. It's the government, our parents, our children, our neighbors. If we get stuck, we can blame it on the evil one, or sometimes we even blame it on God. Yet in marriage, we are often quick to blame our spouses.

It is time to take responsibility. You may say it's 75 percent your spouse's fault. Well, I don't care if it's 99 percent your spouse's fault! In every conflict you hold at least some responsibility, even if it's just a small fraction. Remember it takes two people to fight. So take responsibility for:

- your part,
- your emotions,
- your attitude,
- your words,
- your actions.

As you talk about your piece of the conflict, be sure to use "I" statements (such as "I feel," "I thought," "I did"). In too many fights couples fall into blaming "you" statements ("You said," "You made me," "You did"). All this does is trigger their defensiveness and escalate the conflict. So if you really want a healthy fight, take responsibility.

Set Up Fight Rules

Conflicts can quickly escalate from an opportunity to strengthen a relationship into something ugly where harmful things are said and done. The purpose of a fight is to enhance a relationship, not to win. To accomplish this, many couples have developed "fight rules." These are guidelines to follow to keep a conflict under control. Below are six rules that couples have found most hopeful.

- Choose a good time and place. Avoid conflict when either of you is too tired, stressed, or angry. Also, avoid conflicts in public or in front of your children.
- Show respect. How you fight is more important than whether you are right. So attack the problem, not the person. And never hit below the belt.
- Stick to one issue at a time. It's easy for one issue to lead to another. Soon you are overwhelmed with too much data involving too many issues. This increases tension, reducing the chance that anything gets resolved!
- Stay in the present. Leave the past in the past. If it was talked about and resolved, then don't bring it up again. Becoming trapped in the past doesn't lead to change in the present.
- Don't interrupt. It's rude and doesn't allow for your spouse to be heard. Listen to your spouse carefully until he or she is finished, then ask your spouse to listen to you.
- Call a time-out if needed. Unfortunately conflicts can escalate. When this happens, call a time-out and each of you spend some time alone before resuming your fight.

Keep Calm

We read in the Bible that we should "be quick to listen, slow to speak and slow to become angry" (James 1:19). In any conflict what you say and do can either be a blanket or gasoline. When a fire is just starting, a blanket can smother the flames while a can of gasoline can cause an explosion that sends it out of control. Be a blanket and do all you can to de-escalate any conflict that is getting out of control.

The more upset you get, the faster your pulse goes. As your heart beats harder, your breathing speeds up and your blood does not get fully oxygenated. Without enough oxygen, your brain does not think as clearly and irrational conflicts are more common. So slow down, breathe deeply, and keep calm.

Take a break.

Take a bath.

Take a walk.

Take a nap.

Also, do what you can to soothe and relax your spouse. Speak softly, listen, and be positive. Prayer is another major calming strategy. Consider praying together before and after addressing each conflict. It is surprising how an honest prayer can quickly set your conflict in context.

Resolve

Many conflicts seem never ending; they recycle over and over. Every fight needs an ending, for this is where closure and clean up take place. To not reach some form of resolution is to fail in your conflict. So here are the three main methods of resolution.

• Accommodation. This is where you say, "I'll change."

• Acceptance. Here you say, "I'll accept that you won't change."

• Compromise. This is where you agree, "We'll both change."

Now you have some form of resolution, even if it is temporary. An important part of resolution is to make sure you both understand what you just agreed upon.

What did you just resolve?

What needs to be done next?

Who is going to do what?

When do these things need to be completed?

With resolution you can now move forward.

Evaluate and Debrief

Every fight is a chance to learn more about each other. Professional sports teams watch tapes of the game they just played to evaluate what they did right and where they need to improve. After each conflict you should try the same thing.

Here are 10 questions that will help you improve your fights and draw closer together.

1. How well did you listen?
2. How honest were you?
3. Did you say anything you wish you hadn't?
4. Did you take responsibility for your part?
5. Did you obey your fight rules?
6. What did you do which made the situation worse?
7. How flexible were you?
8. What did you learn from this fight?
9. How would you handle yourself differently next time?
10. How can you communicate your love in spite of your disagreement?

Use your responses to debrief with each other. Learn from your mistakes and learn how to be a more loving fighter.

Make Up

When Tami and I were first married, we had a running joke that we loved a good fight because it was so much fun to make up. The bigger the fight the greater the making up. This is the key to a good fight.

First of all apologize for wrong thoughts, attitudes, words, or actions. Don't wait for your spouse to initiate the apology. Too many times a husband or wife waits for the other to start. You take the first step and your partner will follow. Ken Sande, in his book *The Peacemaker,* suggests that you forgive each other with the four promises of forgiveness.

- I will no longer dwell on this incident.
- I will not bring up this incident again and use it against you.
- I will not talk to others about this incident.
- I will not allow this incident to stand between us or hinder our relationship.

Finally, both of you initiate positive, loving behavior. If you love each other, show it. Grow up and make up.

Encourage each other and say nice things. Conflict can be exhausting and leave a person feeling fragile. Take care of each other. Do something fun and relaxing. Enjoy your time together as you reconnect. Be gentle and compassionate. One of the best ways to end a fight is with a hug. Not a forceful, sexual, or halfhearted hug, but a genuine, tender, I-love-you-with-all-my-heart hug. A genuine hug is a symbol of emotional and physical reunion that reminds you that you are both on the same team.

Making up sure does feel nice.

Wrap Up

Couples do not always agree. You have a great resolution, but your spouse thinks his or hers is better—much better. You feel strongly about your point of view, but your spouse digs in and feels equally strong about his or her point of view (which happens to be totally opposite from yours).

Words fly.

Quills extend.

Conflict escalates.

You've been there before and so have I. The challenge is, how do you work through your conflict when there are two porcupines living in the same house?

The secret is simple: Be more concerned with whether you are hurting your spouse than whether he or she is hurting you. As you gently and respectfully lay down your quills, most spouses will do the same. This does not mean you should avoid conflicts; it means you should fight in a way that does not hurt your spouse. In so doing, the anger and frustration will subside. The issues will be resolved. You will understand each other more. And you will find that even a fight can bring you closer together.

Hallway Projects

1. Discuss one of the top six fights you have had lately and what you both could do to resolve it.

2. Think through the latest fight with your spouse and go below the surface. What underlying needs do you think was present? Which of these do you think was present with your partner?

3. Agree upon at least six fight rules. Write them down and post them someplace where you both can be reminded of them.

4. List any conflicts you have had during of your marriage that have not yet been resolved. Talk to your spouse about which method of resolution you will apply to each conflict: accommodation, acceptance, or compromise.

5. Go together to your favorite restaurant and share your answers (not your spouse's) to the 10 evaluation questions about your last big fight. Your spouse may then share his or her answers, if desired.

6. Come up with at least 10 ways to make up after a fight. Try a few of them after your next conflict.

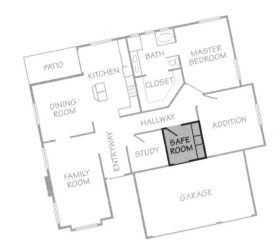

8

THE SAFE ROOM
Crisis Projects

A storm was coming.

I was almost eight years old and the school had sent us home early. They told us to find a safe room in our houses where there were no windows, lie down on the floor, and wait for the winds to pass. Oregon doesn't have a lot of bad wind storms. I didn't know a lot about hurricanes or typhoons or cyclones, but I had seen *The Wizard of Oz,* so I knew a bad storm could lift up a house and take it far away.

I was the only one home. Mom and Dad wouldn't return for another three hours. I sat down at the kitchen table to have some milk and cookies. Then the storm hit. The wind blew so hard that the house shook; the windows rattled, and I prayed. The wind howled louder and louder until I put my fingers in my ears. I peeked carefully out of the kitchen window and saw a tree come crashing to the ground with shingles, leaves, and debris violently swirling around. The lights flickered, then went out. Now I was really getting nervous.

I frantically ran through our house looking for a safe place, but every room had windows. The storm was getting worse and we had no safe room!

Suddenly there was a knock at the door. It was Mrs. Schultz, the neighbor. "Are you okay?" she asked.

"I can't find a safe room."

"Come with me," she said. "We have a safe room." She took my hand and we went to her house.

Every house needs a safe room, a place to go when storms and struggles blow into your life. These places may also be called storm cellars or disaster shelters or panic rooms. Whatever you call them, their purpose is to help you make it safely through emergencies.

When Tami and I built our house, we designed a pantry in the very middle of the main floor. This could be our safe room. It is well stocked with bottled water, canned food, candles, blankets, flashlights, a first aid kit, and anything we might need in an emergency.

When storms come our way, we will be prepared.

Crisis Togetherness

Life rarely goes the way we dream it will go. It is full of twists and turns. Around every corner there is a potential surprise: Some bring celebration and some bring crisis.

Marriage, like life, rarely goes as smoothly as you think it should. No matter how well you plan and prepare, events happen that catch you off guard. You get a hint at what's to come in most weddings. Years go into dreaming about the perfect wedding ceremony, and many months are painstakingly spent orchestrating every detail. When that special day finally arrives, the bride and groom are caught in the magic of the moment. Then inevitably something goes wrong. Most weddings I have attended have had their unplanned occurrences—everything from babies crying and off-key singers to fainting brides and complete electrical outages.

This is how marriages begin.

You try so hard to plan perfection, but ultimately you must admit that there is much in life that we are unable to control. Marriage is full of unexpected crises—some seem small and relatively manageable, but others shake you to your core.

These difficulties can either destroy your marriage or make it stronger. They can either pull you apart or drive you together.

Unfortunately the greater the crisis, the more likely it will cause your relationship to stumble. The times you both need closeness, communication, and compassion the most are often the times you are most likely to withdraw into yourselves, leaving each of you to experience your grief, fear, or confusion alone.

Crises come in many sizes and flavors. Sooner or later they will strike your relationship. Though it is nearly impossible to be fully prepared, it is important to talk about the most common crises and discuss how you would handle them if they struck you. So here are nine serious opportunities to practice crisis togetherness.

Death of a Loved One

It was a simple game.

It was four-year-old Jason's favorite game to play with his mother.

As soon as the mail truck came to their quiet cul-de-sac, his mother would say "Go" and Jason would run as fast as his little legs could move, across the yard, across the street, to the mailbox.

The first one there won.

His mother always gave Jason a head start, and Jason was always the first to the box. Once there he would raise his hands above his head in glee and shout, "I won! I won!"

One bright, spring day his mother said, "Go," and Jason took his last run across the yard, across the street. But he never made it to the mailbox. By the time his mother saw the car speeding into the cul-de-sac, it was too late.

The screech of brakes.

The thud of the small head on the asphalt.

His mother wept as she held her son in her arms as he gasped for breath and faded into unconsciousness.

Jason's father could not forgive his wife for this stupid game. And Jason's mother couldn't forgive herself. Their silent pain tore the relationship apart and two years later they divorced.

It is tragic that within five years of the death of a child, 75 percent of all couples divorce. At a time when a husband and wife need each other more than ever, they build walls around their hearts and carry this unimaginable grief alone.

There are other deaths that are significant blows. The death of a parent is difficult no matter how old you are. But when it is sudden and unexpected, it is a double blow. I can't even imagine life without Mom or Dad.

The death of my grandmother was particularly hard. She once told me that she had prayed for me every day of my life, and she was such a woman of faith that I believe she did. When she died, Tami stood beside me and walked with me and listened to all my stories of Grandma Blanche.

Our children.

Our parents.

Our grandparents.

All these losses affect us. They create a hole, an emptiness, a sorrow that must be shared. The shock, depression, loneliness, anger, regret, pain, and loss must be expressed with someone who can understand. Your spouse is that person. Pulling away either traps you in your grief or hardens your heart in repression and denial.

People never "get over" a significant loss, but they learn how to move on in spite of the empty place they carry for the rest of their lives.

The bottom line is that a couple needs each other to survive the death of a loved one or any other painful loss. Losses of many types can create a crisis: a loss of security, friendship, job, dreams, trust, or valuables. Any of these hold the potential to shake us up personally and thereby affect our marriage.

Psychological Difficulties

"Something is wrong with my husband," said the frantic woman on the other end of the phone.

"What are his symptoms?" I asked.

"He won't get out of bed. He just lies there, staring at the ceiling. When I try to talk to him, all he says is, 'I can't do it. I can't do it.' He keeps repeating that line over and over."

Scott had always been a hard worker, but finally the pressure of a demanding job pushed him to the limit and he had a breakdown. From that point on Scott was never quite the same. Instead of being strong and confident, he was now somewhat fragile and unsure of himself. He found a new job at half the salary and slept a lot more than ever before.

But Catelyn stood beside him and in time he laughed again and regained much of what he had lost. This couple stood together through the emotional crisis. It is tough, but Catelyn developed a patience, sensitivity, and strength that she never thought possible. Meanwhile, Scott sensed her love, and this provided an atmosphere conducive to recovery.

Emotional struggles are difficult to understand and anticipate, yet as our culture becomes more hurried and complex, they impact a growing number of couples. Here are some of the most common emotional struggles.

- Anxiety
- Obsessive-compulsive disorder
- Phobias
- Panic attacks
- Bipolar disorder
- Depression
- Attention deficit disorder
- Anger management issues
- Post-traumatic stress disorder
- Schizophrenia
- Psychosis or dementia

These are just a few that can strike any couple and stretch their togetherness. If your spouse struggles with emotional difficulties, come alongside them and show them what practical love really looks like. If you struggle mentally or emotionally, get professional help and pray for your partner's patience.

The good news is that with proper treatment, personal determination, and a supportive spouse, most emotional difficulties will improve. The frustration is that they rarely improve as quickly as you would like.

Health Problems

I rushed forward to smash the racquetball against the wall. But instead of a hit, I heard my ankle rip, and I collapsed facedown on the shiny wooden floor. For the next three months I was in a full-length leg cast.

Tami says those were three of the hardest months of our marriage. I was basically useless, and much of what I usually did now fell onto her shoulders. Illness or injury places a great deal of extra stress on a marriage, and at times this stress can be overwhelming.

On Tuesday Janice was fine.

On Wednesday she had a bad headache.

On Thursday an aneurysm ruptured in her brain and the right side of her body was completely paralyzed.

Janice was an attractive, talented 32-year-old woman who was now permanently strapped into a wheelchair—unable to talk clearly, unable to feed herself, unable to go to the bathroom without help.

"You don't deserve this," she said to Rich in a drawn-out slur that took a moment or two to comprehend. "This isn't fair to you. Put me in a care facility and forget about me. Go on with your life."

Rich ran his fingers through her once-silky blonde hair that had lost most of its luster. Tears collected in the corners of his eyes. "You are my love and I don't know why God allowed this, but I will always be by your side."

That is crisis togetherness.

During the next five years, Janice and Rich developed a sense of togetherness they had never known before. Then in the middle of a frosty December night, she died.

At the funeral Rich spoke of the difficulties since the aneurysm. Then he said, "But somehow it was all worth it, for we grew closer in the past five years than during any other time of our marriage."

Maybe you can avoid the challenges of disease and accident, but no living being can avoid aging. As time passes, one's body is not as fast or flexible or resilient as it once was. This is the human condition, and as we grow older we run the risk of more health problems than when we were younger.

I love to watch elderly couples who have been married over the long haul. These are the ones who have held tight through the rough weather of life and learned that crisis creates character. For them health problems are like rain in Oregon: You just get used to it. You carry a big umbrella and huddle close and try to stay as dry as possible.

Challenges of Children

Children are full of life and joy, but they can drive their parents crazy. They can also break your heart. When they present challenges it is important that parents stand together as a team. Some challenges such as trouble with homework, whining, picky eating, resisting bedtime, or sibling rivalry are fairly normal. These issues need to be dealt with. Though they are stress-producing, they rarely escalate into a full-blown crisis. Most couples form some point of agreement, develop a plan, and follow through with a consistent means of implementation.

Yet as children become teenagers, parenting often becomes more difficult. Parents frequently come to me saying, "What happened to my wonderful little girl?" or "My son used to be so good." Suddenly small frustrations become large problems and in many families you have a crisis. Some challenges are hard, but others can seem overwhelming. Issues such as violence, school truancy, defiance and rebellion, sexual acting out, drugs and alcohol, or trouble with the law can push a couple to the break-ing point.

Sixteen-year-old Jonny took the family car without permission for a joy ride with a few friends. The boys drank a short case of beer and drove much too fast. The car rolled and all the boys ended up in the hospital. The injuries were only minor, but the car was totaled. A week later Jonny's parents found a baggie of marijuana in his bedroom. His father felt this was the last straw and believed his son needed serious consequences. Jonny's mother wanted her son to have one more chance. Soon the par-ents were more upset at each other than at their son.

Far too often the challenges of raising a teen become a crisis for the marriage. Parenting concerns soon stretch beyond the family with issues that have significant academic, safety, legal, moral, and social ramifica-tions. At this point, each parent often sees the problem differently and confronts the other instead of the child. When a couple does not parent as a team, everybody suffers—especially the children.

Whether you are dealing with issues of sexual abuse or mental handi-caps, eating disorders or rejection of faith, your children need to see you working together as a couple. Avoid taking opposing sides in front of your children. If you disagree, discuss it privately. If one sees the situation as a crisis and the other doesn't, be sensitive to each other.

Regardless of the situation, remember two things: (1) You both love your children even if you see things differently; (2) Working together doesn't have to mean total agreement.

Financial Struggles

"Please don't try to stop me," Rob said without emotion. "This is the only way. The life insurance benefits will pay off our massive debt and provide enough to take care of Heidi for the rest of her life."

I couldn't believe that Rob was seriously contemplating suicide. Yet there had to be more to this. "What does Heidi say about your debt?" I asked.

"She doesn't know half of it," Rob said. "I didn't want to worry her with all the ugly details, so I just kept it to myself."

That was Rob's biggest mistake!

When you keep a struggle to yourself, it tends to get worse. What is crushing to one can usually be managed by two. Financial difficulties can strike any couple. When your security is threatened, it is easy to panic. Yet this sort of challenge can also be a reminder that those things that money can't buy are the things that matter most.

After our talk, Rob went home and was totally honest with Heidi. Together they developed a plan to deal with their massive debt. For the next three years they lived on the bare necessities. They sold much of what they had. They planted a garden, discontinued the newspaper, rode the bus, shopped at thrift stores, and took on second jobs.

What seemed like a hopeless situation became a gift where this couple learned that when you stand together, with God's help, you can handle almost anything. Too often we believe money can somehow buy happiness, but it can't.

At the same time, finances are a part of life and financial struggles can easily create a crisis in your relationship. We live in a world that seems to have a price tag on almost everything. But don't let finances damage your relationship. Natural disasters, job loss, unwise investments, overspending, theft, or costly medical emergencies can happen to any couple. All these can bring about a financial crisis, but they can all be survived. These are a part of life. Jesus reminds us not to even worry about food or clothing. "Seek first his kingdom and his righteousness, and all these things will be given to you as well. Therefore do not worry about tomorrow, for tomorrow will worry about itself" (Matthew 6:33-34a).

Disappointments and Hurts

We all have certain expectations of what a good marriage is all about. Maybe you think a husband should take care of all the financial needs; that he should be hardworking, even-tempered, and incredibly romantic.

At the same time he should be a strong spiritual leader, a nurturing father, and a highly respected figure in the community. Maybe your image of a wife is that she keeps a spotless home, that she should be in great physical shape, never get stressed, and be able to do miracles with a limited budget. She should also be your best friend, a gracious hostess, and a sexual partner more tantalizing than you ever thought possible.

Most of us enter marriage with unrealistic expectations. You want your spouse to fulfill all your dreams. You rarely stop to think about how you don't fulfill your spouse's dreams. You need to focus on how you are going to be the best spouse possible, and in so doing you hope your spouse will do the same.

Yet regardless of how hard you try to meet each other's expectations, there will still be disappointments and hurts. It's like learning how to dance together. The music might be beautiful and the setting inspiring, but the two dancers are human. Periodically they miss a beat, fall out of rhythm, and step on each other's toes. At first they apologize and ignore the pain. But it happens again and then again. Soon you want off the dance floor. You just want the pain to stop.

Marriage is a dance full of these disappointments and hurts. For some couples these difficulties come as an unimaginable shock that causes the first year to have more divorces than any other season of marriage. For other couples the pain accumulates until it feels overwhelming. These disappointments and hurts come in many shapes.

- Insensitivity
- Impatience
- Forgetfulness
- Annoying or offensive habits
- Cruel words
- Selfishness
- Laziness
- Broken promises
- Unattained dreams
- Unresolved conflicts

You might not even be aware of what you've done and how you have stepped on the toes and heart of the one you love. But regardless of your intent, there is damage. To ignore, defend, or minimize your guilt only makes things worse. To speak gently, respectfully, and humbly, taking responsibility, can calm the spirit of the one you have stepped upon and reassure him or her that you truly meant no harm. Though there is no way to avoid all disappointments and hurts, you can trust again. And in time, believing the best about each other, you'll learn to dance together with grace and love.

Addictions

"He's a great husband," Shauna said, "except when he drinks. Then he gets mean and stupid."

"All I want is a few beers with my buddies after work."

"If it were just a few beers, I could handle it," said Shauna. "But he drinks until he can hardly walk straight. I can't take it anymore."

Addictions destroy marriage.

One of the biggest problems with addictions is that they can become so consuming, frequently taking priority over your spouse. This is especially true of the "Tragic Five":

- Alcohol
- Drugs
- Sex/pornography
- Gambling
- Eating disorders

These compulsive behaviors usually involve dishonesty and coverups. They break the trust between partners and make the compulsion the center of the addicted person's life.

"So what are you going to choose?" I said to Dwaine. "You can't have both. Your wife needs to know what is most important to you: your pornography or her. If you choose your pornography, she will leave. If you choose her, she will do anything she can to help you beat your addiction."

Dwaine looked at me with tears in his eyes. "I love my wife, and this is probably the dumbest decision I've ever made, but I can't live without my pornography."

"Oh yes, you can," I said.

"Maybe I don't want to," he said. "I've made my decision, so shut up and leave me alone."

It doesn't have to be this way.

Addictions are never easy, and when handled alone they can be overwhelming, frequently destroying you and your marriage. But when a couple stands together, seeks appropriate help, and leans on God, a seemingly hopeless situation can be turned around.

But it doesn't take just the "Tragic Five" to bring about a marital crisis. There are other, lesser addictions that can also lead to a crisis if allowed to get out of control. An obsession with shopping, work, television, computers, hobbies, or sports can also be very hard on a relationship.

Balance is always important. When any of these seems more important to you than your spouse, you are in trouble. You are out of balance, headed for a crisis and ready to fall.

Moral Failures

"All have sinned and fall short of the glory of God," writes Paul in his letter to the Romans (3:23). We are all flawed and we have all done wrong. In fact we have all done things we hope nobody ever discovers.

In nineteenth-century England, Sir Arthur Conan Doyle, the author of the Sherlock Holmes stories, decided to play a practical joke. Late one night he sent telegrams to five or six of the most prominent citizens of London. The message was simple:

I HAVE DISCOVERED ALL STOP FLEE LONDON IMMEDIATELY OR EVERYTHING WILL BE PRINTED IN TOMORROW MORNINGS NEWSPAPER STOP

Early the next morning Doyle went out to visit the recipients of his telegram. But to his surprise none of them were home, for sometime during the night each had mysteriously disappeared from the city.

We have all had moral failures, but certain moral failures within marriage can quickly escalate into a crisis. The greatest of these are:

- untruthfulness,
- unfaithfulness,
- unlawfulness,
- unresponsiveness.

Each of these involves a breach of trust and some level of hardness of heart. They involve a betrayal and with every betrayal there is a consequence. Damage has been done to the relationship—damage which must be acknowledged, dealt with, healed, and forgiven. If this damage is ignored, denied, or minimized, it could destroy your marriage. But if the damage is sensitively dealt with, these crises can actually strengthen a relationship.

Pain from outside a marriage is difficult, but pain from our own spouse can tear your heart out. But if the offending partner humbly takes responsibility, genuinely seeks forgiveness, and faithfully rebuilds trust, then even a moral failure can draw a couple closer.

Midlife Challenges

It is amazing how many marriages fall apart at midlife. You might expect that after 20 or more years of marriage there would be enough maturity, experience, wisdom, and commitment to face the most difficult situations. But that does not seem to be so. The number of midlife divorces is staggering.

Yet this does not need to be the case.

The solution is simple. If you are willing to evaluate and do a remodel, the second half of your marriage has all the potential to be more fulfilling than the first half. This does not need to be a crisis, but it does need to be a time to set some new goals. Here are 12 that will get your home back into great condition.

- Refocus on each other (rather than children or occupations).
- Reject and let go of your past disappointments.
- Relax with who you are (and how your body is changing).
- Rejoice in what you have.
- Renew your romance and love life.
- Restore your communication.
- Resolve your anger and ongoing conflicts.
- Rebuild your friendship with each other.
- Reevaluate your spiritual pilgrimage.
- Readjust to changing roles.
- Reconnect with hobbies, interests, and what you find fun.
- Reinvent your marriage.

At the mid-marriage mark you have built a lot of memories with each other, some good and some not-so-good. Don't let the challenges of midlife create a crisis in your marriage; instead let it trigger a recommitment to the love that first brought you together. This is indeed the best time in marriage for both of you.

Don't miss the opportunity.

Don't get distracted by fantasies and foolishness.

Don't throw away all you have.

Wrap Up

Every marriage will face a number of crises during its life span. These crises can make you bitter or angry, pulling you apart from each other and possibly even destroying your marriage. On the other hand these difficult and seemingly overwhelming crises can have a positive impact. Often it is the crises of life that draw a couple closest, rather than the times where everything is smooth and good. In the crises we learn how to trust and forgive; we grow in maturity and sensitivity and compassion; we develop character as we practice love and patience; we deepen our faith in a God who is always there ready to comfort, even if we do not understand how He could allow such pain.

There are many lessons in crisis. It's like the story of the diamond; beauty, strength, and value are developed from the pressures of life. Facing the pressures and crises of life together, hand in hand, will make your marriage into a diamond. Then you will become a glowing beacon that will shine forth as an example to all who know you. And when your time on this earth comes to a close, you will leave a legacy of beauty, strength, and value that will never die.

Safe Room Projects

1. List every crisis you have experienced since you've been married. How have these impacted your relationship with one another?

2. Which of the nine areas of crisis is or would be the hardest with which to deal? Talk together about why this area is the most difficult and how you might deal with it.

3. Chart out any emotional difficulties, health problems, or addictions that have occurred in your family of origin. What would you do if any of these struck your marriage?

4. Discuss how you might handle the normal challenges and the more difficult challenges of children.

5. Write down five times you have hurt the feelings of your spouse. Apologize to him or her and do something to show that you are truly sorry for what you have done.

6. Dress up in your best-looking clothing, wear your best-smelling perfume or cologne, and go out together to your favorite romantic restaurant. Once there, talk about how you can give your marriage the 12-point home remodel explained on page 132.

9

THE PATIO
Aesthetic Projects

There was great potential. It just needed some vision and hard work. Yet in the beginning the French doors of our family room opened onto a pathetically small slab of concrete and an acre of blackberry brambles. There was a stand of fir trees at the back of the property, but little else.

Tami and I sat on our three-foot by three-foot concrete patio, dreaming and talking about what we might do to bring beauty into our backyard. During the next few years we cleared the land, put in a lawn, and planted some trees—a maple, a white pine, a dogwood, a plum, a weeping willow, two eucalyptus, and four cherries. Soon Tami was also creating flower beds with everything from hydrangeas to hostas to honeysuckle. With care and creativity our backyard was transformed into a place of peace and beauty.

Yet our patio still looked pathetic.

To rectify this, my father and I started leveling an area for a larger patio about eight years ago. We built a retaining wall, filled an area with gravel, and laid two thousand pavers outside our family room. It looked great. Tami added her touch by planting strawberries, sunflowers, and nasturtiums around our new patio. Now in the mornings or early evenings Tami and I can sit in our patio chairs and enjoy all the beauty of God's creation. We have two birdfeeders near the patio, which draw hummingbirds, blue jays, sparrows, robins, and chickadees. It's amazing to marvel at the endless cycles of nature from our patio. Every once in a while we get a surprise visitor like a family of deer, a curious raccoon, or a baby rabbit who is frantically looking for its mother. This outdoor room brings us close to nature and allows us to build our aesthetic togetherness.

When you have a home, there are always new projects or improvements. Last Father's Day, Tami gave me an outdoor fireplace for our patio. There was one problem, though: There was no good place for it. But Tami had a solution—expand the patio. So for the past two months, together we have built a wall, leveled more gravel, and laid another nine hundred pavers. Now we have a larger patio with a wonderful place for my outdoor fireplace.

Somehow life is more positive and beautiful when we sit on our own patio together. Everything that is good overwhelms us. It's a place of simplicity and an escape from the hectic pace of life. In our outdoor room we can savor the artistry and grace that surrounds us. We can also enjoy each other and nurture the wonder of aesthetic togetherness.

Aesthetic Togetherness

"Life is difficult," reads the first three words of M. Scott Peck's classic *The Road Less Traveled*. Peck is right, but life is also filled with an amazing amount of beauty.

One of my favorite movies is a charming 1997 Italian film by Roberto Benigni entitled *Life Is Beautiful*. In it, Guido is a devoted Jewish father who created a beautiful life for his wife and young son. But then World War II began, and the Nazis took Guido and his family to a concentration camp. Here they were surrounded by hard work, little food, cruel rules, few freedoms, and harsh conditions. Yet Guido was determined not to allow his wife and son to be crushed by all these difficulties. In the end, Guido's wife and son survived this horrible nightmare because Guido could find beauty in the most unlikely of places.

In marriage there are hard times and difficulties. It is easy to allow the frustrations, challenges, and disappointments of everyday life to distract you from all the beauty surrounding you. Sometimes it's even hard to see it. Aesthetic togetherness involves sharing beauty with each other. This togetherness will enrich your life and your marriage.

Aesthetic togetherness brightens your joy, heightens your closeness, and intensifies your love. The more the two of you focus on aesthetic togetherness, the better even the most difficult seasons of your marriage will appear. So gaze into each other's eyes and together toast a lifestyle that honors beauty.

Aesthetic togetherness can be elusive, but it doesn't have to be. In order to appreciate this form of togetherness to its fullest you need to have a strategy. Moving to Tahiti is one way to discover beauty, but for most of us that's not possible. Part one of a proactive strategy to build aesthetic togetherness is to recognize the five areas of beauty. Part two involves a willingness to commit to five responses to beauty. As you combine these two parts, your marriage will become more beautiful.

There are many facets and forms of beauty touching every one of the five senses. But for a couple to be healthy and growing, that couple must develop an attitude of being open to all that is beautiful. If you have this attitude and your spouse doesn't, don't be discouraged. An attitude toward the beautiful is so contagious that if you focus on it and nurture it, sooner or later your spouse will succumb to its powerful force.

So check your attitude.

Open your eyes and ears.

Discover the beauty around you.

Enjoy all five of the following.

The Beauty of Positives

Negativity is ugly. It can destroy a marriage through discouragement. Negativity is like a slap in the face. It pushes your partner away and kills their enthusiasm for the relationship. Far too often I hear things like,

"Nothing will make her happy" or "No matter what I do, it's not good enough."

A negative attitude is dangerous, while a positive attitude is truly a thing of beauty. Chuck Swindoll wrote, "Life is 10 percent what happens to us and 90 percent how we respond to it. Attitude is the single most significant decision I make each day." At every moment of every day you have a choice before you to have a positive or negative attitude. A positive attitude increases happiness, reduces depression, decreases stress, and strengthens your marriage.

I realize that in spite of all the reasons to have a positive attitude, it is not always easy. It takes looking beyond circumstances and feelings. Sometimes circumstances are not very optimistic, and feelings can pull you down.

John's parents died when he was three. For the next 12 years he was bounced between 20 different foster homes. At 16, after a brutal beating by an alcoholic foster father, John ran away.

Ten years later, John was successful businessman with a terrific wife. When I asked him about his difficult childhood he said, "I guess God had some important lessons to teach me. He taught me self-discipline, the importance of hard work, and compassion for kids in difficult situations. Hopefully all these lessons will make me a better husband."

John is a great example of how people can rise above their circumstances and feelings to get a positive attitude. But there are many people with great circumstances and fine feelings who cling to a negative attitude. Enjoying the beauty of positives involves a determination to be positive. Here are 10 ways to be positive:

1. Practice positive attitudes.
2. Repeat positive thoughts.
3. See positive qualities.
4. Speak positive words.
5. Encourage positive actions.
6. Pray positive prayers.
7. Make positive choices.

8. Befriend positive people.

9. Develop positive goals.

10. Live a positive life.

There are always things to complain about. Murphy's Law says that whatever can possibly go wrong will go wrong. All too often this law seems to come true. But an optimistic person has learned to find positives in any situation. He has discovered that optimism has more to do with your focus than with your circumstances. Someone once said that the pessimist complains about the apple's seeds, but the optimist plants them. To find the beauty of the positives, you must choose to focus on the positives. Paul encourages us in Philippians 4:8 to focus on all that is true, noble, right, pure, healthy, graceful, admirable, polite, exceptional, and praiseworthy. If you focus on these things, you can't help but be positive.

The Beauty of Creation

Right now as I write this, I'm lying on a sandy beach in Mexico with Tami by my side. The sun is sparkling on the waves of the sea-green Pacific as pelicans swoop down for their late afternoon catch. Behind us a grove of luscious coconut palm trees sway in a light breeze. Bright red bougainvillea and other exotic flowers make the scene as perfect as this world can offer.

Tami leans over and whispers, "Isn't this beautiful?"

"Absolutely," I reply as I soak in the scenery.

The natural beauty here is unusually spectacular, but wherever you go and wherever you are, there is amazing beauty. My grandfather loved the desert. Tami loves the beach, especially in warm weather. I am content just about anywhere. Even when I was in northern Iceland, near the Arctic Circle, I was surprised at the incredible beauty that surrounded me: the jagged mountains, midnight sun, breathtaking waterfalls, bubbling hot springs, and rocky shorelines.

God has such an awesome imagination that through nature He created beauty in every imaginative form. When I see a clear blue lake, a doe and fawn at the edge of a meadow, or a hillside covered with wildflowers, I long to share it with Tami. I'll say, "Look at this!" or "Did you see that?" Enjoying beauty together makes it more special and draws the two of us even closer.

Sunsets are extra special to the two of us. We love to hold hands and watch the reds and yellows and purples paint magic on the western horizon. Each sunset is uniquely beautiful and breathtaking. We have shared hundreds of sunsets. After each one, we embrace and kiss each other. Often even a picture of a sunset can bring us closer. One year Tami and her mother went to Hawaii together, leaving me behind to watch our three kids. While she was gone, my two boys came down with chicken pox. Tami offered to come home early, but I reassured her that I could handle it. Several days later she sent me a postcard of a spectacular sunset over the beach at Lahina. On the back all she wrote was four simple words, "I'm thinking of you!" Suddenly I felt very close to Tami in spite of the thousands of miles separating us.

So notice the many beauties of nature and share them with each other. Here are 28 of the most beautiful things in nature.

1. Sunrises	15. Bird life
2. Mist	16. Lightning
3. Mountains	17. Storms
4. Waterfalls	18. Beaches
5. Snow	19. Oceans
6. Clouds	20. Coral reefs
7. Rainbows	21. Islands
8. Icebergs	22. Trees
9. Canyons	23. Plants
10. Caves	24. Flowers
11. Jungles	25. Fruit
12. Deserts	26. Seasons
13. Land animals	27. Sunsets
14. Sea animals	28. Night skies

God's natural creation changes from season to season. In the spring, green buds appear on the trees and the music of birds fills the air. Warm showers invite flowers to blossom everywhere—purple crocus, red tulips, yellow daffodils, blue forget-me-nots, and multicolored pansies. In the warm, sunny days of summer, roses and honeysuckle share their sweet scent. Beneath the clear blue skies fruit ripens to a delicious perfection—strawberries, cherries, apricots, peaches, watermelon, and grapes. As the cool evenings of autumn leave their frosty touch on the pumpkins, the trees blaze bright in a burst of glory before their leaves swirl to the ground. The days grow shorter and colder as the clouds hide the winter sun and the seasons end their yearly cycle. Storms sweep the land with angry gusts of wind and sometimes even gentle blankets of snow. Each season is a special delight.

Enjoying the multifaceted beauty of nature together involves sharing your experiences using all five senses. Seeing the full moon stand strong on a canopy of sparking stars during a romantic night. Hearing the morning song of birds outside your bedroom window. The soft touch of your lover's hair on a lazy summer day. The clean smell of the forests after an afternoon walk in the rain. The sweet taste of feeding each other freshly picked strawberries. God gave you five senses to share His beauty with each other.

King David stared into the sparkling night sky over Jerusalem and wrote, "The heavens are telling the glory of God; they are a marvelous display of his craftsmanship" (Psalm 19:1, TLB). I love to sit with Tami on our patio on a clear evening and watch the night sky. The stars twinkle and the moon shines brightly. We are so small and God is so big. Tami and I huddle closer together, sharing our warmth while thanking God for this beautiful creation and each other.

The Beauty of Artistry

Another aspect of aesthetic togetherness is the celebration of the artistic. Art in its purest form is an attempt to duplicate, interpret, reflect, describe, or approximate some aspect of God's creation. Art takes on many forms and mediums. My dictionary defines art as "human works of beauty." Enjoying art side by side with your spouse creates an emotional, intellectual, and aesthetic connectedness.

I don't have much artistic ability, but I enjoy the art and talents of others. Not long ago, Tami and I wandered through a city marketplace at sunset. We stopped to watch a local glassblower form flamingos and dolphins. Then we stood in amazement as a young man painted miniature beach scenes and palm trees. A short time later we listened to street musicians sing romantic ballads accompanied by acoustic guitars. It was a fantastic evening of artistic togetherness.

Art is something to share. Tami and I have found certain movies we love to watch together. Each Christmas Tami and I cuddle close to watch *White Christmas*, *Miracle on 34th Street*, or *The Preacher's Wife*. Movies can provide both recreational and aesthetic togetherness. Good movies, whether classic or recent, can be a fun way to bring you close.

Tami and I both enjoy music, but the styles we appreciate are very different. When we were first married there were only two or three CDs we enjoyed together. Over the years Tami has shared with me her favorites and I have shared mine. Our musical tastes are still quite different, but the CDs we both enjoy now number in the twenties or thirties. Not only have we discovered more CDs we can share, but we also found special songs we now call "our songs." Whenever we hear these songs we are reminded of our love. When we dated, I would sing Tami a classic Beatles song, "I Will," and it became our first song. When we were on our way to the hospital for the birth of our second child, we heard Van Morrison's "Have I Told You Lately That I Love You." It instantly became one of our songs. Since then we have added five or six more. These beautiful songs bring us moments of aesthetic togetherness in the midst of our hectic lives. When things get rough, we play one of our songs and all our troubles are eclipsed by our love.

Art builds closeness in so many ways. When I read something beautifully well-written, I yearn to share it with Tami. Reading prose to each other as diverse as George Macdonald's *Phantasies,* F. Scott Fitzgerald's *The Great Gatsby,* or Pat Conroy's *The Prince of Tides* brings us closer.

Now the problem with artistic beauty is taste. What I find beautiful, Tami may not and vice versa. Certain paintings or photographs that I find inspiring might leave Tami unmoved. I enjoy landscapes and she enjoys floral displays. Yet appreciation of art often takes time and cultivation. You must give it a chance. By taking the time to appreciate what your spouse finds beautiful, you are showing respect for him or her and possibly even broadening your sense of the artistic. Tami enjoys ballet, and for years I insisted that I would never join her in this interest. But then I realized I was missing an opportunity to enhance our togetherness. So I went to *The Nutcracker Suite* with her. I must admit that it was beautiful and that sharing the experience with her was special, but I will never be a fan of ballet. I went because I love to be with my wife, and she says the exposure to culture is good for me.

Sharing artistic beauty lifts you above the ordinary. Find areas of artistry you can share and then fill your life with exploring this type of beauty.

The Beauty of Goodness

There is a beauty in goodness. When we see a young boy help an elderly lady with her packages or a wife being patient with an angry husband, we are impressed. A person who keeps their word is admired. A person who is generous is respected. Someone who shows courage is honored. These traits are recognized as good because they are noble. Goodness takes character and effort. It builds healthy relationships and promotes community.

When I hear of someone cheating on her husband or being verbally abusive to his wife, I am saddened. We live in a world of bad behavior. Goodness provides hope. It is a glimpse of the way things should be. Unfortunately goodness is not as common or popular as it once was. About a year ago I realized that a salesperson had given me a dollar more in change than belonged to me. So I went back and returned the dollar. The salesperson looked at me as if I were crazy.

"Why didn't you just keep it?" she asked.

"Because it wasn't mine," I replied. "Besides that, it wouldn't have been right."

She took the dollar, but acted as if no one had ever returned any money. As I left, a lady approached me with her six-year-old son. "Thank you for returning that dollar. You set the sort of example I want my son to see."

Doing good is truly beautiful!

In a postmodern world that says all values are relative, it is more important than ever to recognize that there are virtues. There are certain qualities that are good, right, and moral. Likewise there are also qualities that are bad, wrong, and immoral. It appears that many have forgotten what is truly good. Here is my list of fifteen basic virtues and values:

1. Honesty	6. Purity	11. Generosity
2. Responsibility	7. Compassion	12. Love
3. Patience	8. Peace	13. Diligence
4. Persistence	9. Faith	14. Respect
5. Self-discipline	10. Humility	15. Courage

Throughout history those who demonstrate these good qualities are held in high esteem. St. Francis of Assisi is known for his humility, George Washington for his honesty, Theodore Roosevelt for his courage, and Mother Teresa for her compassion. Reflecting on these virtues and those who held them brings a couple closer together. It unifies you and your spouse as you share the beauty of moral goodness.

Together enjoy goodness. First, look for it in each other. Encourage virtues and values in your spouse. Compliment him or her. One of the reasons I married Tami is that I saw a sense of goodness and a striving for goodness in her.

Second, look for it in family and friends. My uncle once told me that his father, my grandfather, was the most moral person he had ever known. What a compliment! Highlight the beauty of goodness in those you know. Talk about it with each other and use it as an example of how the two of you would like to be.

Third, look for it everywhere. Discover role models for a good marriage and emulate their strengths. Find goodness in books, history, and current events. Wherever you find it, celebrate it together. Discuss ways you can be better in every possible virtue. John Wesley once said, "Do all the good you can." Let me add: Do all the good you can together. As you share goodness, you will find the beauty of what aesthetic togetherness can offer.

The Beauty of Simplicity

More and more couples are becoming disenchanted with and even angry at the fast-paced, complex world they live in. They yearn for the simple life of a bygone era when there was the time to sit back on a front porch, sip lemonade, and talk about things that matter. To accomplish this goal, many are willing to downsize, simplify, and de-clutter their lifestyle.

A frenzied lifestyle pulls couples apart. It gets you moving faster and faster. Speed kills. It kills intimacy, conversation, and simplicity. At this fast pace it becomes difficult, if not impossible, to discover or appreciate any aspect of beauty. As you race to reach your goals, meet your obligations, or just keep up, aesthetic togetherness becomes a nice thought and nothing more. Simplicity allows you to slow down so you can enjoy each other and everything else. Without simplicity you become confused, chaotic, and overwhelmed.

Stu and Tauni were tired of the rat race. They both quit their high-paying, prestigious jobs and sold their large suburban home. Stu explained that their lifestyle was hurting their marriage. "We are so busy earning money that we don't have time for each other."

So they simplified. They bought a much smaller house out in the country, got less demanding jobs, and learned to live without all the extras that had once cluttered their lives. "This was one of the best things we've ever done," said Tauni. "Now we have time to relax and love and live."

Simplicity says that less is more. Yet in our materialistic world we gather, collect, consume, and expand. An old bumper sticker reads, "He who dies with the most toys wins."

What a lie.

Our culture is obsessed with stuff. It occupies our days and dreams. Stuff may be attractive, but it rarely satisfies for very long. Stuff grows. It requires care and repair. It must be stored and organized and protected. Stuff often owns you as much as you own it. Most of us have far more stuff than we need, but for some strange reason we still want more. Henry David Thoreau wrote, "Our life is frittered away by detail. Simplify. Simplify. Simplify." To prove his commitment to his own advice, he lived alone in a small cabin out in the woods near Walden Pond for a full year.

It's time to embrace the beauty of simplicity. So start by considering some of the areas you might de-clutter.

- Your home
- Your schedule
- Your mind
- Your priorities
- Your work
- Your play
- Your faith
- Your time together
- Your time apart
- Your life

Beauty is at its best in the simple—holding hands, a single red rose, a bowl of freshly picked strawberries, a walk along the beach. The best things in life and in marriage are usually the simple things. Love grows in simplicity, when life is calm and peaceful. With all the noise and activity that surrounds us, our love can get lost. I frequently encourage couples to try an audio-visual fast. Turn off your television, radio, CD player, and computer. Enjoy the quiet and solitude. Listen to the wind, the birds, the one you love, and the voice of God. As the psalmist wrote, "Be still, and know that I am God" (Psalm 46:10). Solitude is a place where positives are pondered, beauty is enjoyed, goodness is celebrated, togetherness is built, and simplicity is embraced.

Simplicity is a beautiful thing and it will bring beautiful things into your marriage. But you need to be willing to let go of the "doing" and "getting," so you can discover the joy of "being." As the two of you accomplish this, you will find a deeper love, a deeper appreciation, and a deeper sense of aesthetic togetherness.

Five Responses to Beauty

We are surrounded by beauty. Yet we race through life only half noting our surroundings. We need the beauty of life to pull us above the difficulties and drudgery of everyday existence. If we let it, beauty will touch our soul. It will make us a better husband or wife. It will give us a better, richer, closer marriage.

Aesthetic togetherness is something that every couple enjoys immensely when they experience it. The problem is that most couples don't experience it nearly as often as they wish.

Why?

Because they don't have a strategy or method to respond to beauty. Here are five strategies for building aesthetic togetherness.

Strategy #1: Seek beauty.

Jesus said, "Seek and you will find" (Matthew 7:7). This is true of many things, especially of beauty. If you don't seek it you may not find it even if it is all around you. Every day you can find at least a few examples in each of the five areas of beauty—a positive statement by your spouse, a wonderful landscape, an inspiring song, an act of goodness, a simple moment of silence.

Search for beauty together. Searching for all five areas can make your marriage an adventure. When you are looking for beauty, it's amazing how much you can find. Suddenly life is not as dull or difficult as you thought. Suddenly your marriage is reenergized with the freshness of new love. Every moment together is now a pleasure.

It is also interesting that as you seek beauty around you, you find it in each other. Here are a few ways to find beauty in each other.

- Discover positives in your spouse's personality.
- See God's hand in your spouse's smile.
- Note a talent you had taken for granted.
- Find goodness in so much that your spouse does.
- Enjoy the simplicity of just being together.

Strategy #2: Acknowledge beauty.

Once you have found beauty, recognize it and talk to each other about it. When I see two or three deer gazing near the creek in our backyard, I get Tami so we can watch together. When I hear one of "our songs," I let her know. When I discover something good, I yearn to share it with her.

Last Valentine's Day, Tami and I went to a great party. On the invitation there were several romantic tips to take on the way to the restaurant where the party was held. One of the tips was to share 18.5 positives about each other.

"You probably can't think of 18.5 positives about me," said Tami.

"Of course I can," I insisted. "In fact, I can come up with 185 positives."

For the next half hour I got to acknowledge 185 positives about Tami. It was fun and Tami thought it terrific. After the party she responded by acknowledging 185 positives about me.

Something special happens when a couple acknowledges beauty with each other. They really do draw closer.

Strategy #3: Embrace beauty.

Jim and Jen took a class on Japanese Tea Ceremony. It took place in a beautiful garden in Portland. To prepare for the ceremony each student was to focus on a tree. I mean really focus. The goal was to embrace the beauty around you; to do this you had to absorb what you saw. They were to study its shape and size; follow its outline and dwell on its symmetry or asymmetry; examine the trunk, limbs, and leaves; and consider the texture and color of each part, noticing the various shadings and hues.

"During the first five minutes I thought I was going to be bored to death," said Jim. "But then I started seeing all sorts of detail that I had never noticed before. I began to see levels of beauty that I had always skimmed over as if they were never there."

Embracing beauty involves taking the time and effort to dig below the surface. Together you can absorb aesthetic togetherness in any number of ways. Embracing beauty means:

- If it's positive—praise it.
- If it's natural—explore it.
- It it's artistic—enjoy it.
- If it's good—celebrate it.
- If it's simple—admire it.

Strategy #4: Appreciate beauty.

Beauty needs to be appreciated. To seek it, acknowledge it, and embrace it without appreciating it is not allowing beauty to touch your heart. As a couple appreciates beauty together, they become emotionally and intellectually intertwined.

A grateful heart fosters an attitude toward life that is both rewarding and contagious. Gratefulness for beauty leads toward gratefulness for each other, which in turn strengthens love and commitment. It also ultimately directs us toward gratefulness for God.

Beauty is so special and meaningful. It adds color to a black-and-white world. It adds spice to a bland plate of food. It adds a soundtrack to an action-packed movie. You can survive without beauty, but everything is so much more enjoyable and memorable with it. Therefore:

Applaud it!

Rejoice in it!

Thank God for it!

Strategy #5: Treasure beauty.

When I was 10, I collected rocks. Not just any rocks, but beautiful rocks such as agates, quartz, and topaz. I kept my special rocks in a wooden box, hidden in the back of my closet so my brothers and sisters wouldn't take them. I protected my collection, but if anyone wanted to see it, I'd pull out my precious box and set the stones before their curious eyes. I treasured my collection. Whether hidden in my closet or held in my hand, it was not forgotten.

Beauty is something that should be treasured. The lovely things of life should be shared, rehearsed, and remembered. Too often we live in the present and forget all the beauty we have experienced. With one rainy day we forget all the warmth and wonder of a sunny summer. We need to nurture our memory so all the attractive aspects of our past do not fade. By treasuring beauty it maintains its glory and power in spite of dark clouds. It gives us hope and encouragement when life becomes difficult.

I love to remember the beauty Tami and I have shared: the laughter of our children, the full moon over an open field, the music of *Phantom of the Opera*, the kindness of our friends, the simplicity of a single rose in a soda bottle. When life is tough or we are frustrated with each other, just the mention of these can bring a smile to both our faces. We treasure these images of beauty by storing them away in our memory for those moments when they are needed.

Memory is a marvel. It is a box where we can place thousands of beautiful stones for safekeeping. Then anytime later we can pull out our treasure and be reminded of the beauty we once experienced. Together we can relish the memory and, in spite of our current pain, difficulty, or confusion, we are transported into a time and place where the loveliness of life surpasses all else.

Store away memories of the positive, natural, artistic, good, and simple beauties of everyday existence. If you could place just one of these stones into memory each day, then within a year you would accumulate a great treasure. And within 10 years you would be wealthy beyond your grandest imagination. Build your treasure and then treasure your beauty. In doing so, you will have accumulated a source of aesthetic togetherness that will enhance your joy, increase your faith, and strengthen your marriage.

Wrap Up

It had been a miserable year!

Greg had lost his job. Evie had lost her mother. They both lost their home because they could not make the mortgage payments. They moved into a small apartment with their two young children. Greg's car was stolen. Evie's identity was taken.

Nothing was going their way.

A friend asked, "How are the two of you doing with your difficulties?"

Greg responded, "God is good."

"But what about everything that has gone wrong this last year?"

Greg stared at his friend and quoted from Habakkuk 3:17-18, "Though the fig tree does not bud and there are no grapes on the vines, though the olive crop fails and the fields produce no food, though there are no sheep in the pen and no cattle in the stalls, yet I will rejoice in the LORD, I will be joyful in God my Savior."

"But how can you rejoice when—"

"Joy is an attitude," interrupted Greg. "It has to do with what you focus on. Evie and I choose to focus on all that is good and beautiful. In any situation your response is based on your attitude, and we are committed to a positive one."

Aesthetic togetherness brings joy, and joy draws us closer to the incredible beauty that surrounds us each and every day.

When I was 10, I stood in a creek bed with my grandfather and he showed me how to find gold. He dug a shovelful of mud from the bank and placed it in a miner's pan. Filling it with water, he gently rotated and swirled the water in such a way that within a few minutes all that was left was a trace of black sand.

"Look closely," Grandpa said.

As I did, I saw a thin line of golden sparkles on the edge of the sand. "Wow," is all I could say.

"Isn't it beautiful," he said. "And to think that most people look at this hillside and only see dirt, when in reality it's full of golden sparkles."

I shall never forget the lesson I learned that day.

No matter how dark, ugly, or commonplace your situation might be, there is beauty right around the corner. In the darkest night, there is the hope of a starry sky. During the ugliest storm, there is the joy of a colorful rainbow. On the most common seashore, there is the excitement of the perfect shell.

Hold hands with each other, while you open your mind, your senses, and your heart. Side by side be amazed at:

- all that is positive,
- all that God has created,
- all that is tastefully artistic,
- all that is truly good,
- all that sparkles in its simplicity.

Patio Projects

1. Each of you name two positive qualities about each of the following.

   > Your life
   > Your spouse
   > Your marriage
   > Your friends and family
   > Your country

2. Spend a day together discovering as many aspects of nature's beauty as possible. Go to a park, a beach, a forest, a zoo, a garden, or anywhere God's creation is evident. Slow down and absorb all you experience. Make a list of your discoveries and put it somewhere special where you can review it together in the future.

3. Spend an evening sharing your favorite music with each other. Select three songs or CDs that you both enjoy. Then snuggle

together on your couch surrounded by that special music that can bring you closer.

4. Separately make a list of five virtues and values which are most important to you. Beside each quality write the name of anyone you know who possesses these admired traits. Then get together to share the five qualities and those who have them. Talk about specific examples of times you have seen or heard these individuals demonstrate goodness.

5. Take a walk together in the area around your house or apartment and talk about how the two of you can slow down and simplify your life. During the next week implement at least one of these ideas.

6. Set aside an afternoon and side by side seek an area of beauty. Then together figure out how to acknowledge, embrace, appreciate, and treasure what you have just found. Write down what you have just done and stash it in a place where you can revisit it in a year.

10

THE MASTER BEDROOM
Sexual Projects

We love our master bedroom.

It is comfortable, relaxing, and romantic. It is our place to escape the children, chores, and challenges of life so we can focus solely on each other. When we want to be private with our conversation or intimate with our physical relationship, this is where we go. Our bedroom has areas set aside for each of these purposes—a sitting area with a wicker loveseat and a resting area with a queen-sized bed. It also has a fireplace, a dresser, two nightstands with crystal lamps, a quilt rack, a CD player, and plenty of candles.

We probably spend more time sleeping in this room than anything else, and while sleeping is important, it is romance that truly sets this room apart. We have never built a fire in the fireplace, but Tami has filled that space with 12 large scented candles of varying heights, which fill the room with a warm glow and a delightful smell when lit. I place a romantic CD in the player, Tami slips into something from Victoria's Secret, and we fall onto the bed, wrapped in each other's arms.

Years ago Tami and I committed to go to bed at the same time and also to go to bed early enough that we didn't fall asleep as soon as our heads hit the pillow. By doing this, we have created the perfect opportunity to reconnect after a hectic day and rebuild our sense of togetherness. This is a wonderful reminder that the two of us are one. We try to set aside some quality time every night just before we go to sleep in order to talk and laugh, share our hearts and expectations, give shoulder and foot rubs, cuddle and spoon and kiss.

This is a time to lie in each other's arms, stare into each other's eyes, and hear each other's dreams. Yet far too many couples wear themselves out before they get to the bedroom. Therefore, all they have is the leftovers of the day. Instead of a positive, exciting time of sharing and intimacy, they drag themselves through tired communication and tired sex. No wonder sexual togetherness is frequently filled with more frustration than joy. Don't let your bedroom become tired or boring.

Tami is always coming up with new ideas to redecorate our bedroom. They rarely involve big changes, but it amazes me how the little things she does can brighten and freshen up the bedroom. She might get a new bedspread, make new curtains, rearrange the candles, or repaint a wall. One evening I walked into a bedroom of pink twinkle lights. Another night the room was filled with freshly cut flowers from our garden and a bed sprinkled with rose petals.

The bedroom should be a place of love. It is the primary room where you express and explore your sexual togetherness. It is a room of gentleness and arousal, a place where you can communicate at an intimate level how much you love each other and how committed you are to a lifetime of togetherness.

Sexual Togetherness

The church service was almost over when an usher tapped me on the shoulder and motioned for me to follow him.

"A couple needs to talk to you," he whispered.

Julie and Tom were standing in a corner of the church lobby. She was crying, and he appeared frustrated. I spoke with them and discovered that they truly loved each other, but they were emotionally disconnected. She felt lonely and he felt unimportant. As we spoke, I asked, "When was the last time you were sexually intimate?"

They both stared at me with blushing faces that seemed to say, "You can't ask that in church. And besides, we hardly know you."

Suddenly it hit me that there are some questions I can ask easily in my office, but I need to be careful asking them other places. Each person seems to have a different level of sensitivity in terms of talking about sexuality. And it's not unusual that even in a marriage, a husband and wife will approach this topic differently. Some people are anxious or embarrassed or uncomfortable with sex. They might see it as an obligation, unnecessary, or something you just tolerate. At the opposite end of the spectrum are those who are obsessed and captivated by sex. They place it on a pedestal and see it as the solution to every marital problem. To either demonize or deify sex is not healthy. The following are some reasons individuals might view sex from these extremes.

- Family background
- Childhood memories
- Personal experience
- Body image
- Personality
- Hormone levels
- Self-confidence
- Accuracy of information

Sexual togetherness can be one of the most positive and enjoyable facets of marriage, or it can be one of the most negative and frustrating facets. Most couples have a sensitivity about sexuality that can easily make it problematic. Any of the eight areas listed above can affect our perception of sex; therefore, it shouldn't have surprised me when I discovered that 75 percent of couples who stepped into my office were struggling with some aspect of their sexual connection. One of the most damaging beliefs is: "We are the only ones struggling in this area; everyone else has a great love life." The reality is that in spite of what you might see on television or movies, sooner or later every couple wrestles with building a healthy sexual connection.

For over 20 years of marriage, lovemaking was not emotionally fulfilling for either Robert or Linda. Linda had not been orgasmic since her wedding night. Her gynecologist said there were no physical abnormalities. Because Robert sensed her sexual frustration it undermined his desire. Years had passed and neither spoke of their sexual needs.

As they sat in my office, I asked Linda what would constitute the perfect evening of lovemaking. She listed 12 things she thought would improve their sexual enjoyment. It surprised Robert. She had never mentioned these things to him. He loved his wife, but certain things he had done were offensive to Linda. Other things that would have been arousing to her had never happened.

At home that evening, Robert and Linda walked through her list. For the first time in over 20 years she was orgasmic. All they needed was communication, time, planning, and work.

I hear many complaints about sexuality. The most common frustrations include the following.

- Not enough touching. "My spouse touches me only when interested in lovemaking."
- Not enough cuddling. "My spouse doesn't like to cuddle."
- Not enough lovemaking. "My spouse has a lack of sexual desire and is seldom interested in lovemaking."
- Lack of context. "We have not been getting along and my spouse wants to make love."
- Foreplay too short. "My spouse wants to move right into lovemaking without enough romance and arousal."
- Too rough and/or aggressive. "My spouse is not tender and sometimes hurts me."
- Poor hygiene. "My spouse's lack of cleanliness makes it difficult for me to enjoy lovemaking."
- Too tired. "We always make love at the end of the day and I'm just too exhausted for it to feel like quality time."

- Poor communication. "My spouse doesn't know what arouses me."
- Too tense. "It is hard for me to relax and really enjoy myself during lovemaking."

Generally, sexual togetherness doesn't just happen. It's a process of sensitivity and fine-tuning. If a couple takes the time, their sexual relationship will grow richer. If they do not, it will become an area of disappointment and irritation.

To build togetherness in any area of marriage, you must deal with the various gaps that pull your togetherness apart. Sexuality provides the potential for at least eight challenging and frustrating gaps.

Bridge the Gaps

1. The communication gap: Since this area is so prone to confusion, hurt, and misunderstanding, sexual communication is very important. Yet most couples rarely talk about their physical relationship—their needs, expectations, preferences, fears, and sensitivities. Duane Story and Stanford Kulkin sum it up with: "Communication leads to greater intimacy. Greater intimacy leads to wonderful sex." The bottom line is that good communication is vital to long term sexual fulfillment. If you want to connect you have to communicate.

2. The gender gap: Men and women tend to approach sexuality differently. Most men find that a physical connection opens their heart to emotional closeness. Yet most women need an emotional connection before they are fully interested in opening their body to sexual intimacy. Men and women also have different physiological and hormonal blueprints that can open the door to all sorts of disconnects. One of the great mysteries of life is how men and women can see the same situation so differently.

3. The desire gap: Different individuals have different levels of desire. This might be an issue of gender, age, adrenaline, time of month, visual stimulation, or a number of other issues. Yet when one spouse

has a high desire, it is a setup for difficulties. The challenge is for the high-desire person to communicate their needs without pressuring or manipulating their spouse, while the low-desire person attempts to be sensitive and generous without becoming resentful.

4. The cleanliness gap: Some people are obsessive about their hygiene, while others are quite casual. If cleanliness is important to your spouse, it is selfish, cruel, and insensitive to not clean up. If cleanliness is important to you, be gently direct without embarrassing your spouse. The sense of smell has a major role in triggering or shutting down arousal. Therefore, brush your teeth, shower, bathe, or do whatever you need to do to make your intimate time positive and pleasurable for your partner.

5. The romantic gap: Romance can melt the hearts of most women. It can easily unlock the door to physical intimacies. Without romance, lovemaking seems empty, cold, and loveless. It is romance that makes this connection so wonderful and meaningful. Yet for many men, romance is irrelevant to sexual togetherness. It is a distraction and inconvenience. To most men, it is the actual sexual act that is so wonderful and meaningful. Also, the question of what is romantic is so subjective that without good communication a couple might never bridge this gap.

6. The comfort level gap: Everybody has a different comfort level in terms of sexual expression. Some people feel very comfortable with their bodies and others might have parts of their bodies that they don't feel as comfortable with. Some people feel more comfortable with certain places and times of the day to be intimate, while others are open to anyplace and anytime. There might also be a gap concerning playfulness, experimenting, exploration, and adventure. Some individuals feel very comfortable in trying new thing;, others have found what works best for them and they would rather not stretch beyond that.

7. The initiation gap: How do you let your partner know that you are interested in an intimate connection without them being

turned off or feeling pressured? How do you read the signals that say "I would really like to be intimate" or "If you gave me quality time or positive communication, it could probably lead to something more" or "Right now would just not be a good time to focus on sexual togetherness"? Too often couples miss the messages, and attempts to initiate intimacy become filled with frustration, hurt, rejection, and misunderstanding.

8. The arousal gap: Men can usually be aroused and feel aroused very quickly, regardless of time, setting, or how they're feeling. Women often build toward amorous feelings and are aroused more slowly, with time, setting, and how they're feeling being important parts of the process. Men tend to be aroused more by visual stimuli and direct messages. Most women are aroused by emotional stimuli and subtle, gentle messages. Therefore a seductive negligee and a direct "come-on" might be very arousing to a guy, while a caring conversation and a tender kiss might be what his wife needs.

These gaps can block your sexual togetherness and create significant damage. However, regardless of these gaps, you can have a great sexual relationship. Please don't allow these frustrations to ever cause you to avoid this area or let sex take on a negative connotation. As Drs. Les and Leslie Parrot write in *The Love List*, "Sex is critically important for a quality marriage." It is not the most important aspect of marriage, but it is high on the list. Sex and intimacy go hand in hand in a marriage. When a husband's sexual needs aren't met:

- He feels rejected.
- He gets irritable or impatient or argumentative.
- He either pushes or pulls away.
- He starts looking in places he shouldn't look.

Likewise, when a wife's intimacy needs aren't met:

- She feels lonely.
- She becomes agitated, insecure, and depressed.
- She withdraws emotionally and builds walls.
- She starts emotionally connecting where she shouldn't.

Healthy physical connectedness meets the needs of both sexuality and intimacy. It brings you close and bonds your hearts together in a way that nothing else can do.

The Three G's

Sex was God's idea. As I read through Scripture I discover that sexuality involves "the three G's." First, *sex is good.* The book of Genesis says, "God saw all that he had made, and it was very good" (1:31). Another translation says that it was "excellent in every way." God created sex, and when it is expressed unselfishly within the boundaries of marriage, it is a great thing. Sexual togetherness is one of the most healthy, beautiful, and meaningful aspects of marriage. Yet like so many good things, if it is not expressed within a context of love, it can do more damage than good.

Sex can be a positive protection for your marriage, for God tells us that *sex is glue.* Genesis says: "For this reason a man will leave his father and mother and be united to his wife, and they will become one flesh" (2:24). Sexual expression not only brings a couple together physically, but also emotionally. It imprints each partner on the other's heart and mind. Sexual intimacy is a major protection from outside temptation. When a couple has a positive sexual relationship, they think twice about jeopardizing that trust. They already have a meaningful source of intimacy, and any other, though it may be alluring, is superficial by comparison.

Freely giving yourself to your spouse is a sign of true romance. *Sex is a gift.* The apostle Paul wrote: "The wife's body does not belong to her alone but also to her husband. In the same way, the husband's body does not belong to him alone but also to his wife" (1 Corinthians 7:4). Every sexual act is a gift that says, "I love you. I'm committed to you. I want to give you not only my heart, but everything I am." Sex is an incredible gift because it symbolizes so very much. Wedding vows legalize a marriage, but sexual intimacy consummates a marriage. My dictionary defines *con-*

summate as to complete and fulfill. This is a gift that validates all the hopes and dreams of your relationship together.

Every couple should embrace "the three G's" and make it a priority to connect sexually at least once a week. One couple approached me after hearing about "the three G's" and said, "We think 'the three G's' are great. In fact we think they are so great that we added three more: generous, gentle, and gleeful." This couple understands that you need to make love in a way that shows love. If your sexual time is reduced to guilt, habit, or duty, something is terribly wrong. This is not what God had in mind.

Part of your marriage commitment is to meet each other's needs. The sexual aspects of these needs involve things like playfulness, romance, physical touch, affection, and intimacy. These are not optional parts of a marriage. Therefore, Paul commands married couples, "Do not deprive each other" of sexual relations (1 Corinthians 7:5a). Sexual frustration can produce irritability, insecurity, impatience, and withdrawal. It can also trigger a loss of trust and emotional connection. Kevin Leman writes that "a sexually fulfilled husband will do anything for you."

Yet when a wife just goes through the motions without being emotionally involved, her husband will not be truly fulfilled. Healthy husbands are most fulfilled sexually when their wives are also sexually fulfilled. You can have a marriage without sexual togetherness, but it will not be all that God intended it to be. I do realize that for some individuals, sexuality is a difficult subject. If there has been abuse, exploitation, betrayal, shame, or guilt associated with sex, then there might be a tendency to avoid or limit your intimate connections. Though I want to be sensitive to your struggle—and your spouse needs to display both patience and compassion—this area is crucial to a healthy relationship. Every couple needs to have regular times of sexual connection. Though expectations may frequently vary between different couples, it is not healthy to go longer than 10 days without a sexual connection. There may be exceptions to this rule, but only if the two of you fully agree to a longer time of abstinence for a specific reason.

Communication and Connection

The most important aspect to sexual togetherness is communication. Yet what shocks me as a psychologist is that very few couples talk openly about their intimate relationship. Because of this silence, too many spouses struggle with hurt, confusion, frustration, and lack of sexual fulfillment. Tyler and Haley had been married for 12 years, but talking about sex felt equally awkward to both, so neither shared that they would like more frequent intimate times. They both waited for the other to initiate. Haley believed the man should approach and Tyler didn't want to push his need unless he knew for sure that Haley was interested. For 12 years this couple—who loved each other so much—felt lonely, unwanted, and frustrated in their sexual togetherness. After speaking openly in my office they also discovered that Haley would like more kissing and Tyler would enjoy more passion. This communication opened up their relationship. Haley recently told me that their sexual connections are better than they have ever been.

Positive sexual togetherness involves talking about your needs, expectations, preferences, fears, comfort zones, and sensitivities. Talking brings you closer, and though it might not solve all your sexual struggles, it at least allows you to understand them better. I realize that this may feel uncomfortable, but it will be worth it. In the Garden of Eden, we find that "the two of them, the Man and his Wife, were naked, but they felt no shame" (Genesis 2:25, MSG). Throughout Song of Solomon, Solomon and his wife talk openly to each other about their intimate relationship. They talk about their emotions and desires, their bodies, their kisses and embraces, their lovemaking. In fact in the past, the book seemed so personal that Jewish rabbis recommended that it should only be read by those who were married or over the age of 30. In it the wife says openly to her husband, "Come, my beloved, let us go out into the fields and . . . I will give you my love" (7:11-12, TLB). The husband tells her, "Oh, how delightful you are; how pleasant, O love, for utter delight" (7:6). The wife boasts: "I am my beloved's and I am the one he desires" (7:10).

Sexual togetherness needs to be explored and talked about. Willard Harley explains this by saying, "The key of communication unlocks the doors of ignorance and opens up to each couple the opportunity for sexual compatibility in marriage." The best way to understand one another is to ask questions and listen to the answers. In their book *The Five Love Needs,* Gary and Barbara Rosberg encourage you to become a student of your spouse by asking the following questions:

- "What would show you that I am interested in your sexual needs?"
- "How often do you need sexual intercourse?"
- "What satisfies you most about our sexual relationship?"
- "What do you need me to do more often?"
- "What do you need me to do less often?"
- "What does it mean to you if I initiate sex?"
- "If I am not ready for sex at the same time you are, how can I show that in a way that doesn't make you feel rejected?"

These questions might get you started, but don't be limited by them. Each couple's intimate relationship is personal and unique. It has its own set of questions that need to be asked and answered. So please take the courage to ask, and show the respect to answer. In so doing, your relationship is sure to grow.

Communication leads to connection—a positive, mutually fulfilling, relationship-building connection. This sort of connection needs to happen at least once a week, and each connection at its best should involve six equally important components.

1. Context: A couple's interaction in the 12 hours before lovemaking sets the context for closeness. A kind and caring day opens each other's heart. To feel safe, respected, and loved by your spouse is a wonderful feeling. To let your spouse know he or she is a priority and truly special to you is incredibly romantic. Compliments and quality time set up a context of love that, even if it doesn't lead to sexual intimacy, will deepen the relationship and draw both partners closer. Likewise neglect, rudeness, or conflict

is likely to push partners away from each other and reduce the probability of an intimate encounter.

2. Atmosphere: A romantic atmosphere softens a spouse's heart and reminds him or her of all that is positive about the relationship. Women tend to be most impacted by romance, but men also have their romantic side. Atmosphere is built upon context, but it focuses more on sensory input. Romance must start with kindness, generosity, sensitivity, and love. Yet what makes this atmosphere so powerful and personal is how it is expressed through our five senses. Through sight we may be moved by candlelight, lingerie, flowers, and certain colors. Through hearing we can be placed in an intimate mood via gentle words and romantic music. Caring touches—holding a hand, an arm around a shoulder, a kiss on the cheek, leaning on each other, stroking an arm, running fingers through the hair—can send a powerful message. The taste of a wonderful meal or desert adds a pleasant feeling to any atmosphere. One of the most overlooked senses is that of smell, but many researchers believe that this is the most powerful means of mood-setting. Scented oils or candles, breath mints, perfume, or cologne can send relaxing and arousing subconscious messages to the brain that will impact you for hours.

3. Connection: Men and women frequently approach sexuality so differently. Most women need some form of emotional connection before they are interested in a sexual connection. The most powerful way to make this connection with a woman is through communication. Talking and listening can warm your wife and help her to be more open to you. When a guy shares his heart—his fears, challenges, excitements, and joys—this draws his wife closer. Encouragement and compliments can also enhance this emotional intimacy. There are also times that a simple listening ear and a shoulder to lean on can be more powerful than a thousand words. In a similar way, nonsexual touch can say "I love you. I'm here and you can always count on me." Remember that sex-

ual togetherness is more about relationship than technique. This is the component where you truly touch each other's heart.

4. Foreplay: This is where a couple crosses the line from emotional intimacy to physical intimacy. Set aside at least 10 to 15 minutes for foreplay. This is the area where most men move far too fast and focus too directly on the erogenous zones. Slow down and gently linger over each other's bodies. Many women indicate that this component of sexual togetherness is the most satisfying and arousing. There are three aspects of foreplay which intensify your closeness and need to be carefully nurtured.

   Serious kissing is an art that too many married couples neglect. Here two individuals—body, soul, and spirit—are totally focused on each other. Learn how your spouse likes to be kissed and become a master kisser. Concentrate on the lips, but don't be afraid to explore other places of the body where kisses are enjoyed.

   Serious cuddling is a necessary part of every marriage. Lying in each other's arms, with bodies fit perfectly together, is an amazing pleasure. At times women only want cuddling and nothing more. Yet most men find this so arousing that they yearn for a closer connection.

   Serious caressing allows you to touch and massage each other in a way that truly shows your love. Learn how to give a massage that relaxes and brings you in sync with each other. Start with the neck, shoulder, back, leg, or foot—whatever gives your spouse the most pleasure. Then move gently and lovingly into more intimate areas.

5. Interplay: Here is where arousal reaches its climax. You share your bodies in a union which brings pleasure and closeness which is so extravagant that little else can compare with it. This is truly a spiritual/emotional/physical experience which is sacred and should be protected so as to be exclusive. It is a symbol of unity and commitment. This culminates in an orgasmic release of endorphins and oxytocin at such a level that couples feel

closer and more positive. In fact, orgasmic couples live longer, look younger, stay healthier, feel happier, give more freely, and love more deeply. Interplay involves the opening up of oneself to your spouse in one of the most intense pleasures of life. It is no accident that God reserves this for marriage, for each act of love-making is a reaffirmation of your original wedding vows with your personal pledge of unlimited mutual love. Therefore it is in this physical symbol that your love is attested, relationship enhanced, romance rekindled, and security reinforced. To reduce sexual togetherness to a mere physical act is to miss its entire meaning.

6: Follow-through: Never allow lovemaking to end abruptly or negatively. Whatever occurred or didn't occur in the previous components of intimacy, you want an affirming and loving close to your sexual time. Even if you're frustrated, disappointed, or unsatisfied, thank your spouse for some aspect of your intimate time. These issues are best dealt with later when you are less emotional. Remember that your sexual time is a gift, not an obligation or something you can demand. Be careful about a reaction that triggers embarrassment, shame, or guilt. Instead build up your partner through compliments and encouragement. When one becomes self-conscious about any aspect of sexuality, there is a risk of intimacy withdrawal, lost desire, reduced arousal, and even the possibility of orgasmic difficulties. So after your sexual time, lie in each other's arms thanking your spouse for sharing physically. Tell your partner how much you love and appreciate him or her. Then create closure on this most precious time with a gentle kiss or a prayer—or even both.

Each of these six components is important. To skip or ignore any of them could damage the quality of your sexual togetherness. To practice each of them during every romantic encounter will strengthen your relationship in ways you may have never anticipated.

Wrap Up

Sexual togetherness requires patience and sensitivity to the needs of the spouse. It is not greedy or demanding. Neither is it stingy or manipulative. Sexual togetherness demonstrates that the more given in every area, the healthier and more satisfying the intimate times. As Ed Wheat writes in *Lovelife*, "Every physical union should be a contest to see which partner can out please the other." The joy of this area enhances the strength of every other area of your marriage. So snuggle close and let your romance grow.

Bedroom Projects

1. Sit down together and discuss: Which of the eight sexual gaps do you struggle with the most and which do you struggle with the least?

2. Share your memories of your most wonderful sexual time together.

3. See how long you can kiss. Then go to various romantic places and try to break your kissing record.

4. Turn on some relaxing music and give each other a half-hour back, leg, and foot massage.

5. Talk about Gary and Barbara Rosberg's seven sexual questions. Each of you ask your partner three additional questions that will help you understand each other better.

11

THE ADDITION
Future Projects

Our house is in a constant state of growth and transition. There is always another project—something that will stretch us beyond our floor plan, create new areas, or make better use of what we already have. In the 13 years since we moved into our house we have made a lot of additions. We built a play structure, a tree fort, and a work area in the back of the garage that included shelves, cabinets, a pegboard to hang my tools, and a long carpenter's bench.

Our biggest addition happened when our youngest child was about four. At that point we realized our two boys were so different from each other that each needed his own individual space. So we decided to build another bedroom. Tami and I figured out where to build, drew up a plan, reviewed our budget, and hired a carpenter to turn it into reality. A month later, 160 square feet had been added to our house, and we have never regretted our decision to expand.

Every house needs its dreams. Tami has a dream of building a pergola over the new part of our patio. She can imagine relaxing in an Adirondack chair in the shade of a blooming wisteria that is growing over the top of this structure. She can see the twinkling lights cast their magical spell as the summer sun nods behind the silhouetted firs. Now I want Tami's dreams to come true. So in two weeks, a few good friends will help me build Tami's pergola. The electricity has already been run beneath the patio and the wisteria is ready to be planted. Hopefully her structure will be finished before the weather turns cold. Then next spring she can sit in her Adirondack chair and enjoy the purple flowers hanging from the beams above her, knowing that dreams can really come true.

Last winter my daughter, Brittany, had a wonderful dream for our house. She wanted to dig out a space under our family room to build an area for teenagers to hang out. I thought this was a great idea, but when we did the research it just wasn't feasible. Brittany was disappointed. I tried to explain that the cost was high, too many support posts needed to be moved, and there was no good place to put a doorway. Even though Brittany's dream didn't work out, I was so happy to see her looking to the future. If we aren't looking forward, we will grow stale and die.

Tami and I periodically sit side by side and talk about additions, improvements, and expansions we might make to the house we have grown to love. We've dreamed of building a 12-by-16-foot guest house in our backyard. Or putting together a small, rustic-looking garden shed. Or remodeling our bonus room above the garage into an apartment for our parents or someone in need. Looking forward to the future together is fun and exciting. It breathes life into our relationship and brings us closer. I strongly believe that a couple who dreams together is more likely to have a future together.

Future Togetherness

"The world is going to hell in a handbasket!" said Mr. Jones.

"You don't know who you can trust anymore," replied Mr. Wagner.

"Prices keep going up," continued Mr. Jones, "and people's morals keep going down."

"Everybody just grows old and dies. I hate the future," complained Mr. Wagner. "It's just one more thing to worry about."

It's been several years since I overheard this conversation, but it's as current as this morning. The future makes a lot of people nervous because it is such a great unknown. James wrote that no one knows what will happen in the future (James 4:14). Remember, Jesus said, "Do not worry about tomorrow, for tomorrow will worry about itself. Each day has enough trouble of its own" (Matthew 6:34).

Some people see the future as a place of anxiety, confusion, or despair. Others see it as full of hope, excitement, and opportunity. But however you see it, your future has great power. Recently, somebody said to me that the future has more power over who we are than our past. The future pulls us forward. The future determines who you will be and often shapes who you are.

The future, in many ways, is what you make it. It is a great adventure. The future is like a vast ocean full of surprises. You chart a route across the sea, not knowing exactly what the weather holds. There might be clear sailing or typhoons. You might not be able to control the storms and catastrophes of life, but you can position yourself where your boat does not sink. The biggest danger on this journey is not choosing a course. As someone once said, "Most people aim at nothing and they usually hit it." Here are twelve potential growth areas for your future.

1. Educational
2. Financial
3. Professional
4. Spiritual
5. Personal
6. Marital
7. Parental
8. Physical
9. Intellectual
10. Emotional
11. Social
12. Recreational

Couples who don't proactively plan their future are likely to look back with regret. Couples who look to the future and develop a strategy for making it meaningful are drawn closer together. In the book of Jeremiah God declares, "I know the plans I have for you . . . plans to prosper you and not to harm you, plans to give you hope and a future" (29:11). The future is an adventure, and to make the most of this adventure you must consider the following four concepts: Vision, Dreams, Goals, and Legacies.

Vision

Many years ago Albert Einstein, one of the most brilliant people of the twentieth century, was riding a train to New York City. As the ticket taker approached him, he couldn't find his ticket.

"Don't worry about it, Dr. Einstein," said the ticket taker. "We all know who you are."

Twenty minutes later the ticket taker returned through the railroad car only to find Einstein crawling about on the floor frantically looking for his lost ticket.

"Don't worry about it," the ticket taker repeated. "We trust you."

Einstein looked at the young man in utter frustration. "You don't understand. This isn't a matter of trust, it's a matter of direction. I need to find that ticket because I forgot where I'm going."

Vision is all about direction. Too many people wander through life aimlessly, not sure where they're going. Too many couples move through marriage clueless, not sure of where they want to go or confused as to how to get there. If Tami and I wish to take a vacation, one of the first things we talk about is where and when. Without a shared vision, we risk either working against each other, going around in circles, or not even getting started. The famous writer Antoine de Saint-Exupéry wrote, "Love does not consist in gazing at each other, but in looking together in the same direction." Now that's the crux of a shared vision.

Every couple needs a vision, and one of the best ways to express this vision is through a mission statement. This gives you a shared perspective for your future. To establish a mission statement for your marriage is easy. In fact, it is critical to not make it too long or complicated. Together get away from the distractions of life, to a place where you can discuss and define what is most meaningful to you as a couple. Identify your priorities and passions, and then set your direction. As you're writing, remember the following five words.

- Clear. Easy enough for a 12-year-old to understand.
- Concise. No more than two sentences.

- Simple. Elementary enough to be recited by memory.
- Significant. So important that it will make a true difference in your life and world.
- Unifying. Reflective of a combined vision both of you unconditionally support.

A shared vision for your marriage brings you closer. It also provides meaning and purpose. In Viktor Frankl's book *Man's Search for Meaning,* he writes that without a purpose life becomes meaningless. Without a purpose we move into boredom and depression and emotional/intellectual/spiritual death. Vision gives life not only a direction but also a purpose. If a couple can discover a mutual direction and together pursue it, the payoff is beyond words.

Jeff and Michelle were unhappy with their marriage. It's not that they weren't committed to each other; it's just that something was missing. They had great communication and few conflicts. They both had good jobs and had recently built their dream house. On the outside everything looked perfect, but on the inside the two of them felt frustrated.

One morning Michelle asked Jeff, "Where do you want to be in five years?"

Out of that simple question came weeks of probing conversation. Soon they discovered that the direction they were headed as a couple was more the result of circumstance and comfort than of any serious planning. So they sat down and developed a vision of their future togetherness. They discussed their talents and abilities along with their values and passions. Side by side they crafted a marriage statement that involved exploring full-time Christian service.

After years of no clear direction, Jeff and Michelle felt closer than ever. They sold their home, quit their jobs, and began working for an orphanage in Mexico. With this unifying vision they felt their marriage had gained a deeper meaning. It now had that missing piece.

Most marriage mission statements aren't so drastic. Here are some that have started various couples on a journey to future togetherness:

- Together we wish to be the most effective parents we can possibly be—raising healthy, godly children who want to have a positive relationship with both of us as long as we live.
- We wish to encourage every married couple we know to have a healthy and loving marriage.
- Side by side we commit ourselves to loving God and loving our neighbors.
- We will support each other's dreams, doing all we can to help, encourage, and bring each dream to reality.
- We will help each other be better people. In so doing we aim to continually grow in character, in faith, in love, in wisdom, in simplicity, and in contentment.

Out of vision comes a mission, and out of a mission comes direction and meaning. Many couples are like the Hobbits in J. R. R. Tolkien's *Lord of the Rings* trilogy. They like a comfortable life with a warm bed and plenty to eat. They are satisfied to live in the here and now. But as Frodo Baggins discovered, there is a great adventure awaiting you. All you need to do is open your eyes and step beyond the ordinary. That is when vision can become reality and dreams can come true.

Dreams

Justin and Brittany had been friends since the second grade. They started dating in high school and got married shortly after graduating from college. Two years later Justin noticed that Brittany was growing sullen and withdrawn.

"Are you upset with me?" Justin asked.

"No," she said. "You're wonderful, but I've always had a dream of going to graduate school in Europe. It just hit me that it'll never happen."

"Why not?"

"It's just not possible."

"But if this is still important to you, we can figure out how to make it happen."

A year later Brittany and Justin moved to Europe where Brittany enrolled in the graduate school of her dreams.

Justin was determined to help Brittany make her dream come true. Because of this, her appreciation of him skyrocketed and their togetherness became better than ever.

Without dreams, something inside of you dies. You need dreams to grow, to love, to live. You need your dreams to be excited about life, and your spouse also needs their own dreams to spark their excitement. Part of your job as a caring mate is to encourage and help your partner to turn dreams into reality. Your spouse's is to do the same with you. In any relationship you can either kill or kindle each other's dreams. Here are seven things that kill dreams.

1. Thinking too small
2. Procrastination
3. Poor planning
4. Fear
5. Laziness
6. Distraction
7. Negativity and criticism

Sometimes you kill your own dreams, sometimes others kill them. The death of a dream frequently leads to grief, disappointment, depression, anger, or even despair. However, doesn't a spouse sometimes have the right or responsibility to kill a partner's dreams?

I don't think so!

But what if the dream seems impossible?

What if the dream might cost you something?

What if the dream scares you?

I don't believe you should ever kill your partner's dreams (unless they are illegal, immoral, or unsafe). Yet I do believe that you might need to help reevaluate, reposition, or reshape your spouse's dream.

Don't take away your spouse's dream; just help him or her develop a better dream. Killing a dream is like killing a part of a person's being. This might become something held against you for life.

Some dreams probably need to be revisited—if you wish to be a singer but can't carry a tune, for instance. Or if you wish to play football but have shattered knees. Aspirations need to be modified if you wish to own a Porsche but are broke.

But most dreams can be acknowledged and affirmed. They might just need to be tweaked a bit to make them work. Somebody once said that nobody has the right to rain on anybody else's dreams. So rather than squash Tami's dreams, I want to encourage them. Dreams really can come true and if you don't do the best to help your spouse achieve their dreams, you miss a powerful opportunity to make them happy. Here are seven things that kindle dreams.

1. Permission to dream
2. Passion and excitement
3. Determination
4. Positive self-talk
5. Visualizing success
6. Interest by others
7. Encouragement

You have your dreams and your partner has his or hers. Supporting each other's dreams is crucial to a fulfilling marriage, but most couples don't know each other's dreams. When we were first married, Tami had a dream of designing and building our own house. After a number of years this dream came true. Then she dreamed of a flower garden with hundreds of types of flowers. I didn't even know there were that many different types that could grow in Oregon. Now our yard blooms February through November. Those were two dreams that I got to help Tami turn into reality. In the process, I discovered that sharing in her dreams allowed me to share in her joy. But dreams don't have to come true to bring happiness. Sometimes just dreaming and sharing those dreams with each other brings joy.

Tami has other dreams that haven't yet come true. Someday she'd like to take piano lessons, help needy children, and travel to Australia. These three dreams can happen.

I know a woman who made a list of a hundred dreams on her twenty-first birthday. Some were big and some were small. (Number 16: Visit the White House. Number 37: Water-ski. Number 42: Hang glide. Number 56: Eat escargot. Number 59: See a play on Broadway. Number 80: Climb the Eiffel Tower. Number 98: Read *War and Peace*.) Her goal was to accomplish two or three of her dreams each year.

Twenty years have flown by and this woman has now crossed off more than 50 dreams from her list. Her husband has been very supportive of her first 50 dreams and together they look forward to fulfilling the next 50.

Know your dreams.

Know your partner's dreams.

Neil Clark Warren writes in his book *The Triumphant Marriage* that learning to dream together is critical. Sometimes these together dreams involve accepting your partner's dream. Tami's dream of designing and building our own house soon became my dream. Merging dreams is magical. So together Tami and I share dreams of children, travel, and helping others.

I dare couples to dream together. Dream big. Dream outside the box. Often couples don't dream because they fear they'll be disappointed, but I'm disappointed when couples don't dream. Without a dream a couple would not marry or build a family or decorate their home. Without dreams the world would have less beauty and more poverty, less laughter and more pain, less peace and more injustice. As Robert Kennedy once said, "Some men see things as they are and say, 'Why?' I dream of things that never were and say, 'Why not?'"

Dream often.

Dream courageously.

Dream lovingly.

Dream together.

As you do this, your world will enlarge and your relationship will grow. Dreams give your marriage a spark, and with that spark it is amazing what marvelous fireworks might be ignited. Let me share with you some wonderful quotes on dreams:

- "If you don't have dreams, you don't have anything." (Jim Morris in the movie *The Rookie*)
- "All our dreams can come true, if we have the courage to pursue them." (Walt Disney)
- "The future belongs to those who believe in the beauty of their dreams." (Eleanor Roosevelt)
- "Cherish your visions and your dreams, as they are the . . . blueprints of your ultimate achievements." (Napoleon Hill)
- "It may be those who do most, dream most." (Stephen Leacock)
- "We grow by dreams." (Woodrow Wilson)
- "Help others achieve their dreams and you will achieve yours." (Les Brown)

Goals

During the 1860s Jules Verne wrote about traveling around the moon.

In 1901, H. G. Wells published a book entitled *The First Man on the Moon.*

On May 25, 1961, President John F. Kennedy announced, "I believe this nation should commit itself to achieving the goal, before this decade is out, of landing a man on the moon and returning him safely to earth."

Impossible!

Ridiculous!

Too expensive!

Too dangerous!

During the next eight years many scoffed at such a fantastic goal. But many others pushed and worked and cheered until on July 24, 1969 Neil Armstrong became the first person to step foot on the moon.

Here is an example of a dream that became a goal, and a goal that ultimately became a reality. Dreams and goals are in many ways the flip side of the same coin, but there are some significant differences. Napoleon Hill wrote, "A goal is a dream with deadline." Goals in general are more defined than dreams, and thus they are one step closer to reality. A dream is general, while goals are more specific. Hopefully your dreams will turn into your goals.

To be a success in any area of life you must set goals, and marriage is no exception. Your marriage needs goals to help the relationship grow, improve, survive, and be as fulfilling as it can be. Lack of goal setting is self-defeating, for as Bob Richards, a two-time pole vault Olympic gold medalist, says, "You hit no higher than you aim."

Alfonso and Keeley were both spenders and after five years of marriage their finances were a disaster. They met with a financial counselor and together set a goal to be out of debt in three years. They made a strict budget and agreed to not use their credit cards during this period. They also agreed to eliminate "extra" expenditures immediately.

No cable TV.

No newspapers or magazines.

No soda pop or coffee drinks.

No new CDs or DVDs.

No purchases over one hundred dollars unless critical.

Giving up these things was hard, but this couple was determined. Three years later Alfonso and Keeley met their goal and the excitement of this success strengthened their marriage. After getting out of debt, they were so energized that they made additional goals that revolutionized their togetherness.

Marian Wright Edelman says to "set goals and work quietly and systematically toward them." It sounds far too simple, but that is all there is to it. What usually gets you into trouble are your fears. A friend once told me that the words "Fear not" appear 365 times in the Bible, exactly one time for each day of the year. Often it is your fears that keep you from moving forward. Here are five of the most common fears.

1. Fear of starting. Beginnings are the hardest. Zig Ziglar says, "You don't have to be great to start, but you have to start to be great." Grit your teeth and do it. Once you get the momentum going, things will be a lot easier.

2. Fear of trying something new. We all have our comfort zones, and when a goal stretches too far beyond the safe and secure, we feel uneasy. But some of the greatest moments of excitement, challenge, and growth involve "stretching out." Abraham had to leave home, Moses had to face the Red Sea, David had to confront the giant, the disciples had to leave all to follow Jesus. Each tried something new, and they never regretted it.

3. Fear of difficulty. Anything that is truly worthwhile takes work. Facing difficulty forces you to grow and mature. It also causes you to appreciate your goal at a deeper level. Things which come easy are frequently not valued. The more difficult a goal, the more it will be remembered and treasured when you have accomplished it.

4. Fear of failure. We all fail every single day. Failure is merely an opportunity to learn. But to many it can be a reason to either not try or give up. Abraham Lincoln kept losing elections, but he wouldn't give up. Thomas Edison couldn't find the right elements for the electric lightbulb, but he kept on trying. Ernest Hemmingway was rejected time after time by publishers, but he refused to quit. The Beatles couldn't get a record company to take them seriously, but they continued to play. Each of these examples would not allow fear to stop them.

5. Fear of modifying. If you are off course, you make an adjustment. If you gain new information, you modify your goal. But I am amazed at the number of individuals and couples who are afraid to alter their course once they have started. It is as if once they have chosen a path they believe that not even "hell or high water" will allow them to deviate from that path. How ridiculous! There is nothing wrong with or weak about modifying your goal. In fact most goals need at least one or two readjustments.

So now that you have seen five fears to avoid, let's deal with how you actually accomplish your goal.

1. Write down and post it somewhere you will see it daily.
2. Do your homework and find the best way to meet your goal.
3. Embrace it and make sure you're willing to pay the price to make it reality.
4. Find a picture to remind you of what you're aiming at.
5. Break it down into practical, specific steps of what to do each day and week.
6. Allow yourself to get excited about what you're doing and where you're heading.
7. Consider what might block, discourage, or distract you, then figure out a way around these obstacles.
8. Make each step as fun and exciting as you can.
9. Get a friend to check with you regularly and keep you on track.
10. Surround yourself with those who can and will encourage you.
11. Focus on only one step at a time, without forgetting that each step brings you closer to the finish line.
12. Work on discipline, consistency, and patience.
13. Remember that a setback is not a failure.
14. Reward yourself each step of the way.
15. Think positively, believing that with God's help you can do it.

When I was in graduate school working on my Ph.D. in psychology, I expected to be sitting beside the most intelligent and insightful people I'd ever met. But it just wasn't so! Most of the other students were nice and respectable, but they were ordinary people. What made them different wasn't intellectual brilliance; it was stubborn persistence. Each of these students set his or her sights on a goal and was determined to reach it.

When a person is positive and persistent it is amazing what he or she can accomplish. Remember the children's story about the little engine who could? The train is confronted with a long, steep hill that looks overwhelming, but the engine repeats to itself, "I think I can, I think I can, I think I can," as it slowly climbs the hill. The harder it works, the faster the train goes. The little engine's confidence builds and soon it is saying, "I know I can, I know I can, I know I can." Before long the engine has reached the top of the hill. The moral of the story is clear: With a positive attitude and a persistent effort, people can accomplish a lot more than they think they can.

Individual goals are great. They provide a chance for you to come alongside your spouse to support, help, and encourage him or her. To have a fulfilling life I believe every person needs individual goals. Likewise, to have a forward-moving marriage every couple needs shared goals. It's exciting how much more you can accomplish when you plan, focus, and work together toward a common goal. Without shared goals a relationship falls into a rut of mediocrity and wasted opportunities. Goals give you an intentional life and an intentional marriage. The following are some common goals I have heard from couples.

- Get out of debt.
- Read through the Bible.
- Go on a date once a week.
- Get a better job.
- Lose weight.
- Raise healthy kids.
- Pursue hobbies.
- Go back to school.
- Get closer to God.
- Make peace with someone.

The apostle Paul writes, "Forgetting what is behind and straining toward what is ahead, I press on toward the goal" (Philippians 3:13b–14a). So choose your goals and get excited about them. If they realistically reflect your values and abilities, you might be surprised at how far you can go. It's not always easy but it's always worth it. Even if you don't accomplish exactly what you want, you have enriched your life, improved your marriage, and strengthened your togetherness. So as Tom Bradley says, "Never give up. Keep your thoughts and mind always on the goal."

Legacies

The car came out of nowhere at over 80 miles per hour. The police and paramedics agreed that Jacob died instantly. His wife and three adult children gathered at his funeral to remember a wonderful life and remarkable legacy. But then an unknown woman in a provocative black dress and sunglasses walked in. Heads turned and whispers spread. Suddenly the secret was spoken and his legacy was forever tarnished.

For 35 years Jacob had been a model husband. But for the past year, he had been involved with another woman. He knew it was wrong. He felt guilt and shame, but he didn't end it. The truth stung, leaving hurt and disappointment. Jacob was no longer the faithful husband and fantastic father. His love and good character and everything that was positive about this man was now eclipsed by his moral failure.

If Jacob had a second chance, he would have been stronger and more committed. He would have thought beyond the moment.

Every person leaves a legacy and so does every couple. Some legacies are positive, some fall short of that mark. I frequently ask people about their parents and one of the questions I ask is: What sort of relationship did they have? I love to hear things like:

- They had a wonderful marriage.
- They were a great team.
- She took good care of him.
- He was a true romantic.
- They loved each other.

But way too often I hear a different type of legacy:

- They argued constantly.
- They never touched.
- He was married to his work.
- She had no respect for him.
- I don't think they really liked each other.

Moses writes that the sins of the fathers visit the children to the third and fourth generations (Exodus 20:5). Negative legacies replicate negative legacies. If you have a difficult or dysfunctional marriage, there is a high probability your children will also struggle in their marriages. Likewise, positive legacies tend to birth positive legacies. The better your marriage, the greater the probability your kids will have good marriages. Now none of this is a full guarantee. For those from bad marriages can, through hard work and sincere prayer, overcome their destiny. Unfortunately those from good marriages can, through selfishness or naïveté, have a broken relationship.

Legacies are made up of many things, but at least four of them start with the letter "m": memories, mementos, messages, and ministries.

Memories. We all leave behind memories. Grandma Blanche and I sat on her front porch many times as she shared her memories of my grandfather—stories of how they met and things they did together. Now that Grandma has passed away, I still hold her memories. She remembered him as a good and gracious man with big dreams. How will others remember you when you are gone?

Mementos. In 1632 Shah Jahan wished to leave a legacy of his love to his recently departed wife. Nearly four hundred years later the shimmering white Taj Mahal stands as one of the most beautiful buildings ever built. What a memento of love! Most of us leave some sort of memento behind—a house built together, a necklace he gave her, a quilt she made to warm their bed, items collected, anniversary gifts, souvenirs, keepsakes, or photographs that capture a moment for posterity.

Messages. "How do I love thee? Let me count the ways," wrote Elizabeth Barrett Browning to her husband, Robert. In fact her entire masterpiece, *Sonnets from the Portuguese,* is a collection of love poems about him. Like every couple, you have a story about how you met, obstacles you've overcome, romantic moments, and experiences you've shared. Mark and Diane Button tell their story in a delightful book entitled *The Letter Box.* Then they encourage you to write your own love story in a letter and send it to your children to be opened sometime in the future—maybe on their wedding day or fiftieth anniversary or anytime they need to know about your love. Whether it's a letter, a journal entry, a poem, or an inscription in a book, the messages you write today can travel far into the future.

Ministries. Every Thanksgiving Day, Steve and Jan worked at a soup kitchen in downtown Portland. On Christmas Eve they took blankets and cookies to homeless people. During their 40 years of marriage they sponsored over 25 children in third-world countries, making sure they received food, shelter, education, and medical care. In their local church, side by side, they taught Sunday school to hundreds of kindergartners. This couple left a legacy of ministry that lives far beyond what they ever imagined.

So what sort of legacy are you going to leave? You might not be able to change the past, but you can certainly change the legacy you leave from this day forward. Talk to each other about how you wish to be remembered individually and together. A positive legacy is a priceless gift. Most people would like to leave a legacy that says:

- You loved God.
- You made your marriage the best it could be.
- You took good care of your family.
- You were kind and generous.
- You were a true friend.
- You kept your word.
- You encouraged others.
- You had a great attitude.
- You helped those in need.
- You lived true to your faith.
- You forgave those who wronged you.
- You left this world a bit better than you found it.

Wrap Up

We all need something to look forward to. Without a future we become stuck with no place to go. Oliver Wendell Holmes wrote, "The greatest thing in this world is not so much where we are, but in what direction we are moving."

There is an old story about a man who was losing his memory. He went to his physician to find out what he could do to stop this forgetfulness.

The physician did a thorough examination and responded, "I've discovered the problem, but there is a difficulty. In order to regain your memory, you will lose your sight. So I want you to go home to think about it and talk it over with your wife. Tomorrow you may return to tell me what you wish me to do."

The next morning the man went to his physician. "I've made up my mind. I'd rather lose my memory than my sight."

"Why?"

"It seems much more valuable to see where I'm going," he replied, "than to remember where I've been."

In many ways this is true. It is much more proactive and positive to live in the light of the future than be trapped by the events of the past. The past is rigid, and we must accept it on its own terms. The future is fluid, and we have the power to shape it into an unlimited number of forms.

So set your vision.

Jump into your dreams.

Work on your goals.

And in so doing, the two of you will draw closer and leave a positive legacy.

Addition Projects

1. Go for a drive together past some of your favorite places. Then stop at a coffee shop and write a marriage mission statement. Remember to keep it short and simple.

2. Ask yourself, "What are five dreams of my spouse?" Then ask, "In what ways do I kill and/or kindle my spouse's dreams?" Commit yourself to do more to kindle dreams from now on.

3. Sit down and list 25 dreams that you share as a couple. Don't evaluate or critique them, just list them.

4. Separately write down five goals you would like to accomplish individually in the next year. Then write down five goals you would like to accomplish together in the next year. Then share your different goals with each other.

5. If you were to die today, what sort of legacy would your marriage leave? Discuss with each other ways you can proactively leave a positive legacy through:
   Memories
   Mementos
   Messages
   Ministries

12

THE FOUNDATION
Spiritual Projects

The construction of our dream house began with the foundation. The ground was cleared and excavated. Footings were laid and forms were set. Then the foundation was poured. By looking at this shape, Tami and I could see the footprint of our new home. This was important; all the construction that followed would rest firmly on this base and be built within the limits set by the foundation. Yet once the house is finished, you hardly notice it.

Every once in a while, I go into the crawl space beneath our house to check the pipes or vents. When I do this I am amazed at the size and strength of the concrete walls that hold up our house. While down there, I frequently check it for cracks or leaks. I live on the side of a hill called Spring Mountain, and it was given this name for good reason in that the hillside spouts hundreds of tiny springs. These run together into small underground streams, which put pressure on each foundation that was built in its way.

Our foundation has never sprung a leak, but our neighbors' did. Several years ago, during a heavy winter rain, the water seeped through their foundation and flooded their basement. This couple was not very happy, for damage was done to their family room, bathroom, and a closet. It was really a mess! It's surprising how a weak or faulty foundation can risk the integrity of rooms that might appear to be in perfect shape. As soon as the rains stopped, my neighbors rolled up their sleeves to repair and strengthen their foundation. In the years since this crisis, their foundation has not leaked. Their difficulty was a great reminder for me to make sure I check my foundation regularly for any problems.

I would never build or buy a house without a foundation, but I once knew a couple who would only buy houses without foundations. They would jack the house up, pour a foundation beneath it, and then set it back down. They told me that a house with a solid foundation was worth a lot more. It was less susceptible to termites or dry rot. It was more stable and less likely to develop low spots. It also increased the longevity of the house.

A house without a foundation is neither safe nor secure. Foundations are usually not fancy or attractive; they are simply solid. It is interesting that David frequently referred to God as his rock. In one place he even says, "The LORD is my rock, my fortress and my deliverer" (Psalm 18:2). The descendants of Korah wrote a psalm that says, "God is our refuge and strength" (Psalm 46:1). A good foundation is our rock. It offers us safety, refuge, and strength. I once heard a meteorologist say that when you find yourself in a strong windstorm, get as close to the foundation of your house as possible. That's the safest place to be. So make sure you are close to the rock, and as a couple, remember that the stronger your spiritual togetherness, the firmer your marital foundation.

Spiritual Togetherness

Betsy loved God.

She grew up in a Christian home and took her faith seriously. She read her Bible regularly and was a genuine, compassionate person. When Betsy was 21 she fell in love and married Henry. However, Betsy's family strongly disapproved of the wedding.

Henry was responsible and kindhearted. He was a wonderful man who was deeply committed to Betsy. Yet he was resistant to anything spiritual. He had never been to church and vowed he would never step into a church. Consequently, the two of them were married by a justice of the peace on the steps of the county courthouse with two witnesses, but no family members from either side.

Shortly after their marriage, Betsy realized something was missing. She loved Henry, but their lack of spiritual togetherness left a deep loneliness. Betsy and Henry were married for 30 years and every Sunday Betsy asked, "Would you like to go to church with me this morning?"

"No, thank you," Henry replied. "Not today."

Betsy would smile and go to church alone. In spite of this setback she refused to give up. Each morning she got up early and fixed a fresh pot of coffee. When Henry came to the table, Betsy poured him a steaming cup and read a short devotional aloud. Then she would say, "Henry, if you would please read today's scripture, I could fix the pancakes." Henry would roll his eyes and start reading. That was their pattern until the day Henry went into the hospital and was told he would probably not live longer than a month.

Henry put his arms around Betsy and whispered, "I'm so sorry."

"It's not your fault," she said between sobs.

"Oh, yes it is," he said. "You have been such a great wife, but I have never accepted your faith. I've watched you go to church and listened to your morning devotions and even read from the passages of the Bible that you asked me to. Over the years it all sank in, but I was too stubborn to admit it." At that point Henry opened his heart and let Jesus enter. Henry and Betsy prayed together for the first time in their marriage.

During the next 12 days, this couple talked more openly and connected more deeply than any other time during their marriage. As Henry began to fade from this world, he held Betsy's hand and said, "Read the Twenty-third Psalm."

Betsy nodded her head.

"The LORD is my shepherd, I shall not be in want.
He makes me lie down in green pastures,
he leads me beside quiet waters,
he restores my soul.
He guides me in paths of righteousness
for his name's sake.
Even though I walk
through the valley of the shadow of death,
I will fear no evil . . ."

Henry squeezed Betsy's hand and they looked into each other's eyes. A broad smile crossed his lips as she read on.

". . . for you are with me."

Betsy looked up because Henry's grip had loosened. His lids closed and he was gone.

Betsy loved Henry, but she always knew something was missing. There were nights she cried herself to sleep and Sunday mornings she sat alone at church with a loneliness that she thought might break her heart. In the end it was all worth it, but she wished desperately that they could have begun their spiritual togetherness much earlier.

The spiritual is the most important and influential aspect of who you are. In your marriage it is without question the single element which can make or break your togetherness. It is the foundation of everything else. If it is not solid, sooner or later, you are in trouble. At the end of the Sermon on the Mount, Jesus said, "The rain came down, the streams rose, and the winds blew and beat against that house; yet it did not fall, because it had its foundation on the rock" (Matthew 7:25). If your spiritual foundation is weak or unstable, your whole marriage risks collapse. Yet if it is built on rock, it strengthens every other aspect of your relationship.

To build a firm foundation you must not allow yourself to become focused on irrelevant distractions, temporary concerns, or all the things of little importance that surround us each and every day. Focusing on God pulls us above the insignificant. It gives us purpose and depth. As you move closer to God, He moves closer to you, and in an amazing way, you both begin to move closer to each other. A God-directed relationship has a strength, love, and perseverance that most marriages don't possess. As Solomon, one of the wisest man in the world, said: "Though one may be overpowered, two can defend themselves. A cord of three strands is not quickly broken" (Ecclesiastes 4:12).

The ultimate goal and peak experience of marriage is spiritual togetherness. Anything else reduces the relationship to mediocrity. Comfort, pleasure, compatibility, and fairness have become the goals of many couples. These are not bad goals, but they are superficial, selfish, and impossible to achieve on a consistent basis. It is spiritual togetherness that gives a couple an eternal purpose and stretches them beyond self-absorption. This brings an incredible sense of joy and fulfillment, but, most importantly, it pleases God.

Spiritual togetherness is not some abstract, other-worldly concept. It is a practical, yet miraculous, way of allowing your marriage to be everything God wants it to be. It is how your marriage can meet its powerful potential. Here are 10 ways spiritual togetherness can make a big difference to your marriage.

1. It encourages both of your individual walks with God.
2. It enhances and strengthens every other aspect of togetherness.
3. It pulls down the walls that might have developed between the two of you.
4. It challenges you to become more Christlike to each other and those around you.
5. It improves your communication with each other.
6. It brings you to prayer more often.
7. It deepens your love and respect for each other.
8. It teaches you to forgive each other more quickly.
9. It shows you the joy and humility of servanthood.
10. It keeps you together for the long haul.

Adding a spiritual dimension to your marriage is more than believing in God or living a moral life or going to church regularly. It is intentionally choosing to follow Christ. When Jesus said to His disciples, "Come and follow Me," each of them took action. When Jesus spoke to the church of Laodicea, He said, Here I am! I stand at the door and knock. If anyone hears my voice and opens the door, I will come in" (Revelation 3:20). God is polite. He waits for an invitation into your life and He also waits for an invitation into your marriage. Once He is invited, you can follow Him by practicing these life-changing steps.

Step #1: Seek God.

We live in a supernatural world and are in the midst of a spiritual battle. We may wish to deny, ignore, or argue this point, but its truth remains. In this crazy and sometimes tragic world, it only makes sense to seek God. David's advice to his son Solomon was: "If you seek him, he will be found by you" (1 Chronicles 28:9b). And when you find Him, you will discover things beyond your wildest imagination. So each day, hold your spouse's hand and seek God's:

- presence,
- wisdom,
- guidance,
- hope,
- comfort,
- protection.

And this is just the beginning. I don't understand how any marriage can survive without God. It's like running blind through a maze on a dark, moonless night without a flashlight. Yet with a seeker's heart, God will be your light and His Word will be your map. A marriage without God traps the two of you in a random, narcissistic world with no hope for togetherness in any genuine, lasting form.

To seek God, a couple must open their eyes and ears and all their senses. God is all around us, but we so rarely recognize His presence. Every day He shows us His hand and speaks to us. Yet we are like Elisha's servant described in Second Kings. Early one morning he awoke to find an enormous enemy army approaching his city. In a panic he went to Elisha, who reassured him with, "Don't be afraid. For our army is bigger than theirs!" The servant looked around and must have thought that Elisha had lost it, for the city appeared totally defenseless. That is when Elisha prayed: "Open his eyes and let him see!" (See 2 Kings 6:16-17, TLB.) This time when the servant looked around him, he saw a mighty ring of blazing angels. On that day the servant learned that you must look deeply, for God is always there.

Every day God sends me hundreds of messages—through people, creation, circumstances, intuition, emotion, insight, imagination, details, music, books, Scripture, and a multitude of ways I've never even considered—but I catch only a small fraction of these messages. How full and improved my marriage could be if I only sought God with more energy and vigilance.

H. G. Wells wrote a story entitled *The Country of the Blind,* where the people in a remote valley lost their vision. Over time they all forgot that they couldn't see and even what they were missing. Stumbling, tripping, and bumping into things became a normal way of life. In their minds, what they couldn't see simply didn't exist. Their lives became limited because they stopped seeking and believing in a world of sight and all that world might contain.

Seeking God must be more than a casual, intellectual exercise. The writer of Psalm 42 wrote: "As the deer pants for streams of water, so my soul pants for you, O God. My soul thirsts for God, for the living God" (verses 1-2a). Truly seeking God involves this sort of craving. It consumes you at all times and places. It is a frame of mind, a state of emotion, an approach to life. As we seek Him, we want to see all there is to see with all the brilliance, color, and detail that is possible for our finite senses to absorb. And then realizing there is still more which with determination and perseverance we might be able to see at some future time, we yearn to seek Him more.

So together as we encourage each other to seek God and lean more on Him, we will discover our world opening up in amazing ways. But to keep quiet about spiritual issues can discourage attempts to seek God. As Gary Thomas asks in *Sacred Marriage,* "Rather than letting marriage blunt our spiritual sensitivities, can we use it to awaken our souls in new and profound ways?" Let us cultivate a deep and vibrant faith in our spouse through our conversation. Talking about our desire to seek God promotes an openness about deepening our spiritual togetherness. As your marriage moves closer to God, "In all your ways acknowledge him, and he will make your paths straight" (Proverbs 3:6).

Step #2: Know God.

The more you know about God, the more your mind opens to Him. Yet the more you know God, the more your heart opens to Him. To know God allows you to place everything else in perspective—in your world, in your marriage, in your heart. As Gary and Betsy Ricucci write, "A magnificent marriage begins not with knowing one another but with knowing God." God is the center of all things, and as the people of Jerusalem prayed: "You alone are the LORD. You made the heavens, even the highest heavens, and all their starry host, the earth and all that is on it, the seas and all that is in them. You give life to everything, and the multitudes of heaven worship you" (Nehemiah 9:6). To know the Creator of the universe is to connect with the source of all knowledge and wisdom. What an absolutely amazing thing! The more I know God, the more I learn about myself and how I can love my spouse more effectively.

God wants us to know Him. The psalmist writes: "Give me understanding" (Psalm 119:34). To know God we must start by studying Him and becoming students of every aspect of Him. One might start by *observing His handiwork*. David said that "the heavens declare of the glory of God" (Psalm 19:1). As you look at nature—the night sky, the plant and animal life, the majestic mountains, the crashing ocean waves—you capture a glimpse of God's presence and personality.

Another way of knowing God is by *watching His ways*. Notice how He works in the lives of people. Look for His principles and how to apply them to your life. Listen to people's stories about how God has affected them and what He has taught them. Much of what I have learned, I have learned from the lessons of others. If God blesses certain things, those are what I wish to pursue. Likewise, if certain pathways lead to distress or disaster, I will choose a different road. I want God's ways to be my ways, therefore I will " [walk] only in his paths" (Psalm 119:3, TLB).

One of the most powerful means of knowing God is by *reading His Word*. You might begin by reading the Scriptures alone and then meditating on them. David wrote, "I lie awake at night thinking of You" (Psalm 63:6, TLB). As you read and meditate, encourage your spouse to do likewise. Then share with each other what you have discovered and how it has challenged you. Ask questions and discuss all you have learned.

There is also incredible power in reading Scripture, a devotional, or a book with spiritual influence together. Each month Christian and Alaina read a Christian book to each other. They cuddle up on their sofa at the end of their day and take turns reading. One month they read the Gospel of John, another month it was *Mere Christianity* by C. S. Lewis. Last month they read *Heaven* by Randy Alcorn. Both Christian and Alaina tell me that their reading together is one of their highlights of each day. Grappling with eternal truths pulls us heavenward and builds our spiritual togetherness. Yet one of the difficulties with reading together is finding quality time that is consistent and free of distractions. Knowing God takes concentration, study, and meditation. None of this is easy, but to do it together helps bond your spirits and meld the two of you into one.

To know God also involves exploring His character. God invites us to know Him, and yet He is a great mystery. There is so much about Him that is beyond our comprehension. We will never fully understand Him, for how can a finite mind ever grasp an infinite God? Yet He gives us millions of glimpses through His handiwork, His ways, and His Word. A few of the characteristics worth exploring include the following.

- God is everywhere.
- God knows everything.
- God is wise.
- God is all-powerful.
- God created all things.
- God is light.
- God has no limitations.

- God has no beginning or end.
- God has ultimate control over everything.
- God is absolutely good and perfect.
- God cares intimately about every individual.
- God wants the very best for people.
- God is the most holy judge.
- God is willing to forgive anything.
- God is love.
- God is beautiful and worthy of praise.

The more you know God, the more you will love, respect, and wish to follow Him, both individually and as a couple.

Step #3: Communicate with God.

Prayer connects us with God. If we wish to seek Him and know Him, it only makes sense that we communicate with Him. Most relationship experts will tell you that regular, healthy communication is essential for any two people to grow closer together. Just as this is true with people, so it is true with our relationship with God. If we neglect to talk to and listen to Him, our spiritual self will shrivel and die. Prayer provides us our spiritual strength and nourishment. Without prayer, we are disconnected from God and our lives are no different from those who deny His existence.

Prayer catapults us beyond the ordinary to a world of the amazing and miraculous where you have daily access to supernatural strength, wisdom, guidance, protection, and comfort. As Paul said: "Pray about everything" (Philippians 4:6, TLB) and "Keep on praying" (1 Thessalonians 5:17, TLB). Prayer is a marvelous thing. As one writer said, "Prayer is the key that opens each morning and the bolt that locks up each night." Another saying is "Prayer is the hem which keeps your days from unraveling." Yet prayer is only marvelous when it is used within a relationship with God. Within this context it is a vital aspect of spiritual togetherness, for its power is two-fold: praying *with* our spouse and praying *for* our spouse.

Praying together is more than a prelude to eating or a last resort in times of crisis. It is a message of love to God and each other. Most people will affirm the power of prayer. Yet that strong belief does not seem to translate into strong behavior. Few of us pray as much as we think we should and fewer of us pray regularly with our partners. Yet Dennis and Barbara Rainey insist, in *Two Hearts Praying as One*, "Praying together may be the single most important discipline you and your spouse will ever share."

Praying together can be both frightening and exciting if done with depth and sincerity. Many of us find it easier to pray with almost anyone else other than our spouse. This may be because our partner knows how often we fail to live up to our words and good intentions. As one husband told me, "She's got too much evidence against me." Exposing your soul—with all its brokenness, hypocrisy, and paradoxes—is humbling and embarrassing.

To invite your spouse to join you in your private conversations with God increases your vulnerability. Pouring your heart out to God is an intimate experience. It strips away pride and pretense, leaving you both naked before a holy and loving God. I'm not talking about voicing a list of things you want God to do. I'm talking about praising Him and confessing your failures and submitting your will to His. It is an incredibly freeing experience when together you seek God through your prayers. It shows you that you can be real and still be loved. It leads you both to a more wonderful relationship of greater trust and transparency. Once you break through your fears, praying with each other can bring about the deepest of all forms of togetherness.

If you care about your spouse or your marriage, you will pray for him or her each day. Something pulls you closer as you pray; your thoughts and emotions become more invested in the other person's well-being. Also something pulls your spouse closer to you when he or she knows you are praying. It provides a spiritual link which is not easily broken. As Ruth Bell Graham writes: "I seriously doubt if there would be many divorces among Christians if they took time to kneel in prayer once a day and each pray for each other."

Prayer is the best protection anyone can get for their marriage. It reinforces your spiritual togetherness like nothing else. Therefore each day, pray for these nine areas.

1. Yourself: Pray that you will be the best spouse you can be in words, actions, and attitude.
2. Your marriage: Pray that the two of you will find and maintain a oneness that will bring you closer as each year goes by.
3. Safety: Pray for your spouse's protection from anything that might cause physical, psychological, or financial harm.
4. Health: Pray that your spouse's body would be free from illness, disease, and anything that might undermine the quality of life.
5. Stress: Pray that your spouse will be able to relax and find contentment in all activities.
6. Temptations: Pray that your spouse will overcome temptations in a way that makes him or her strong, humble, loving, and more dependent on God.
7. Fears: Pray that fears will not paralyze or compromise your spouse, but lead to a deeper faith that will bring peace and courage.
8. Dreams: Pray that your spouse's dreams will come true in a way that enriches life and glorifies God.
9. Faith: Pray that your spouse's walk with God will become stronger and stronger, leading to the joy of following Him.

Let praying for your partner become as much a routine in your day as eating a meal or turning on a light. By so doing your spiritual togetherness will blossom into something truly beautiful.

Step #4: Embrace God.

To move close to God ultimately means to embrace Him individually and as a couple. It involves placing all you are into His hands and inviting Him into every nook and cranny of your relationship—your finances, conflicts, disappointments, obsessions, dreams, everything. To embrace God, you must make Him top priority in your life. This establishes your foundation of spiritual togetherness. With God in this primary position, all is submitted to His will. Your marriage must then be firmly in second place. Paul tells men to love their wives like they love their own bodies. The fastest way to destroy your marriage is to neglect these two principles. God must be first; your marriage must be second. Everything else—job, security, hobbies, friends, appearance, possessions, and yes, even children—must be placed below these two.

We live in a culture that says, "It's all about me." To follow this philosophy will crumble your foundation and cause your marriage to collapse. As the old catechism says, "The chief end of man is to glorify God and enjoy Him forever." As we do this individually and in our relationship, we will find that all our needs will be met. We will find a joy that we could never discover apart from God. There are many ways to rise above our selfishness and embrace God. Among them are loving Him, thanking Him, and honoring Him.

All the greatest people in Scripture encourage us to love God. Moses said, "Choose to love the Lord your God and to obey him and to cling to him, for he is your life" (Deuteronomy 30:20, TLB). David says it more emotionally with, "Lord, how I love you!" (Psalm 18:1, TLB). And Jesus puts it all in perspective as He says: "Love the Lord your God with all your heart, soul, and mind. This is the first and greatest commandment" (Matthew 22:37-38, TLB). To genuinely embrace God comes from a love of Him. Just as we warmly, passionately, sincerely embrace our spouses, let us do the same with God.

Love is not passive. To love God, we tell Him and show Him. We include Him in our thoughts and plans. We yearn to be with Him and talk about Him. The same is true of our spouses. If we love them, we do certain things. Sometimes our love is a choice (as with Moses' words), sometimes it's an emotion (as with David), and sometimes it involves our whole being (as with Jesus' words). However we might show it, our mutual love toward God brings our hearts, souls, and minds closer to each other. The more we learn to love God, the more we are capable of expressing our love to each other. For if God is love, what better source to gather more love in order to return it to Him and heap it upon our spouses.

When we love someone, we thank that person and help him or her feel appreciated. God has done so much for us—He created us, loved us, brought the two of us together. Part of embracing Him is to show our thankfulness. David cries out, "O Lord my God, I will give you thanks forever" (Psalm 30:12). Every day I want to thank God for His love, patience, creation, grace, guidance, miracles, mighty works, protection, peace, joy, and much more.

As the two of you thank God together, it reminds you of all the positives around you. There is nothing so positive as a thankful heart. The thankfulness you both direct toward heaven soon overflows onto each other. A positive, appreciative attitude toward each other deepens your love and strengthens your togetherness in all of the 12 areas we have explored in this book.

In addition to loving and thanking God, we honor Him by giving Him our time, our attention, our abilities, and our gifts. Generosity shows honor to God. When we together give to Him, we feel an incredible connection as husband and wife. To give to God or others as a couple involves a sense of unity and teamwork. Generosity creates joy in those giving and those receiving. As we give to God, we learn how to give more graciously and spontaneously and intimately to each other.

Honoring God through our giving to Him together also opens us up to receiving His blessings together. As we give to God, He says: "I will open the windows of heaven for you and pour out a blessing so great you won't have room enough to take it in" (Malachi 3:10, TLB). By giving to God and to each other, we learn the principle of return: the more we give, the more the receiver desires to give back to us. Therefore, as we honor God through our giving, we will find blessings that will deepen our relationship and strengthen our togetherness.

Step #5: Serve God together.
To embrace God, we must be His servants. We must be willing to do it His way and submit ourselves to Him. Serving God is not always easy or

convenient, and we can come up with all sorts of reasons as to why we can't do it. Yet if we take our spiritual lives seriously, excuses are just excuses. For our spiritual lives to be alive and vibrant, our behavior must match our beliefs. As James says: "Faith that doesn't show itself by good works is no faith at all—it is dead and useless" (James 2:17, TLB). Jesus modeled for the world how to serve others, and He reminded us that the first shall be last and the last shall be first. We should all be servants. We can do this in three ways: serve God together, serve each other, and serve others.

When Joshua spoke to his people at Shechem he declared, "As for me and my household, we will serve the LORD" (Joshua 24:15). Serving God side by side is submitting to His will and way. It is the yielding of the finite to the infinite. It is a couple giving themselves to their Creator so He can direct them to their greatest potential. To serve God involves putting aside your schedule and priorities; by so doing you must trust that God's way is best. Only as we fully submit to God can our service be genuine, our lives be fulfilled, and our marriage be eternally meaningful.

All you do can be service to God, if you do it with the right attitude. Many of the painters and composers of the Renaissance wrote on their works "To the glory of God." Service is an attitude. Doing things together for God's glory or pleasure is a wonderful act of service, whether it involves teaching Sunday school together, writing a book together, weeding a garden together, or welcoming a new neighbor together.

Another beautiful way to serve God is by being a servant to your spouse. In its purest form, service is love in action. It involves giving, helping, sacrificing, and temporarily putting aside your desires for those of your spouse. Instead of competing to get it your way, compete to do it your spouse's way. Know your spouse's needs and do everything you can to meet these needs as often as you can. If your spouse needs a glass of water or a break from the kids or a back rub, provide it.

Lisa is a worn-out mother of three special-needs kids. Recently she developed some health problems, and her father passed away. Lisa was on the verge of a nervous breakdown. Her husband stepped beside her, assisting, encouraging, and comforting her. But she needed something more, so he put together a surprise to give her something she had always dreamed of. He arranged for his parents to take care of the children and he took her on a seven-day Caribbean cruise. Now that's service.

Jesus said that loving God was the greatest commandment, but He also said, "The second is like it: 'Love your neighbor as yourself'" (Matthew 22:39). So to love your neighbor means actively reaching out to serve anybody you can—even those who are difficult and make you feel uncomfortable. Throughout Scripture, God tells us that we have an obligation to the sick and needy and anyone less fortunate than us. James writes that true religion means that we must "look after orphans and widows in their distress" (James 1:27).

Together find a way to serve others in your own community. I know a couple who volunteers at their local grade school. Another couple serves meals at a homeless shelter each Thanksgiving and Christmas day. Others take meals to shut-ins, babysit for single mothers, or read to the visually impaired. Each of these activities can be done as an individual, but as a couple they are more powerful, for each spouse and those you are serving. As a couple you may also stretch beyond your community and serve at an even broader level. Together you may sponsor a child through an international relief organization, build a house for Habitat for Humanity, spend a week working at an orphanage in Romania, or get involved in one of hundreds of worldwide opportunities to help others.

Step #6: Reflect God.

If we sincerely seek and serve God we will over time begin to reflect His goodness and character. As a couple you will be seen as positive, kind, and compassionate. When Moses spent time face-to-face with God on Mt. Sinai, his face glowed so bright that people could not look at it. The longer and closer we walk with God, the more we will come to look like Him. Therefore let all you say and do reflect God. As Paul says, "Follow God's example in everything you do" (Ephesians 5:1, TLB) and "Let us not get tired of doing what is right" (Galatians 6:9, TLB).

Reflecting God involves living a life that shines with His virtues. Paul lists nine wonderful virtues that many refer to as the "fruit of the Spirit." What does reflecting God look like?

- Show love when those around are not lovable.
- Have joy when those around are discouraged and discontent.
- Exude peace when those around are anxious.
- Practice patience when those around are hurried and frantic.
- Reach out in kindness when those around are difficult.
- Shine with goodness when those around do evil.
- Stand in faithfulness when those around have no commitment.
- Flow with gentleness when those around are harsh and cruel.
- Demonstrate self-control when those around have none.

Each of these is a choice, but they are choices we can't make without God's help. We are all broken, and without God's healing touch we will fail. Yet as God guides and strengthens us, all things are possible. Therefore, as we reflect these nine virtues to each other and all those we come into contact with, our spiritual togetherness grows strong and our marriage flourishes in a thousand loving and beautiful ways.

Wrap Up

Marriage is a test of your faith. It is a refiner's fire that either draws you closer to God or pushes you away from Him. The only way you can have a truly successful marriage is by trusting and submitting to God.

We live in a world that strives for fun, entertainment, things, comfort, and ease. Yet we soon find, like Solomon, that none of this is satisfying for very long. Jesus says that He came to give us a full and abundant life. He also came to give us a full and abundant marriage. The only way to achieve this is through the foundation of spiritual togetherness and building all else upon this rock-steady base. As Gary Thomas asks in *Sacred Marriage*, "What if God is more concerned with making us holy than with making us happy?" If you seek happiness, you will be left with nothing. But if you seek holiness, you will ultimately find happiness and everything else you ever needed.

Foundation Projects

1. List three ways you could spiritually encourage your spouse.

2. Share your favorite verses or passages of Scripture with each other.

3. Go to a bookstore and find a Christian book that is of interest to both of you. Then commit to reading it together at least two times a week.

4. For one week pray for your spouse every single day by going through each of the 10 areas listed earlier in this chapter.

5. Discuss six ways in which the two of you could serve God together by serving others in your community. Then choose at least one of them that you would be willing to commit to do sometime during the next month.

13

KEEPING IT ALL IN ORDER

"The strength of a nation lies in the houses of its people."
—ABRAHAM LINCOLN

Guys love garages.

This is where they escape and tinker and fix things. This is where they try to keep everything in order. It's kind of like the control room of the house. In most garages there is a workbench and a place to keep the tools. Some guys have a lot of tools and some have just a few. My good friends Dan and Roy have tools for everything. I just have the basics—hammers, saws, clamps, screwdrivers, pliers, wrenches, and a power drill. Shortly after moving into our house, my father came over and said, "Steve, you need a workbench." So over the next couple of weekends he helped me build a workbench and hang up my tools on a pegboard wall. It looked great.

It's amazing how many tools it takes to keep your house in order. Several months ago my boys broke a door. I went to my garage and was able to get the tools I needed to fix it. The longer I've been married, the more things in our house I learn to fix. Every year I expand my collections of tools and every year I learn to repair something new.

Yet sometimes I get stuck. I either don't have the right tool or I'm not exactly sure what to do. As a guy it is often hard to ask for help, but I've learned that if I don't reach out I'll make one of the following mistakes:

- I'll avoid the problem.
- I'll make the problem worse.
- I'll spend a lot more time fixing the problem than I should.

Therefore, I will call a friend to help. Sometimes I ask to borrow his tools. My friends laugh at my tools and say, "When are you going to get some good, heavy-duty tools?" Dan has every tool ever made, and he can fix almost everything. So when he comes over to help, he brings his own tools. He says, "If you're going to do a job, you have to do it right." What he is really saying is that you have to have the right tools and I don't have them. When it comes down to it, I know I need friends like Dan.

Other times I ask to borrow a friend's expertise. Last night my hot water heater went out, so I called Roy. Before the end of the day, Roy had helped me find a new hot water heater and helped me install it. I couldn't have done this job alone, but with Roy's help everything went perfectly. I'm honest enough with myself to know what my strengths and weaknesses are. When I hit a weakness, I call a knowledgeable friend.

Sometimes I can make home repairs by myself and sometimes I can do it with the help of a friend, but there are times I need to call in an expert to do the job for me. Last winter I had to call a furnace repair company to fix my furnace. It was freezing cold, my furnace was dead, and Tami thought some heat would be nice.

I didn't know how to fix a furnace and my friends didn't either. We didn't even know where to start, so I turned to an expert. Within a few days, the repairman had it fixed and our house was as warm and cozy as ever.

Every marriage needs periodic work done on it to keep it healthy. Some of this work you can do yourself. With some of it you are going to need some assistance—healthy friends, a mentor couple, a seminar, a good book, or whatever else can provide you with better tools. Then there are times when you need to call an expert because the situation is just over your head. This is hard for some of us guys to do. Guys need to understand that asking for help does not mean you are less of a man or have failed or are somehow less than competent. What it does mean is that you care about this relationship and are smart enough to know when you are over your head and you have the courage to do something about it. Wives, please realize that seeking professional help is very difficult for your husband. He has to swallow his pride and admit he can't fix everything. To go to an expert—a pastor, counselor, or psychologist—is a big step out of our comfort zone.

The Proper Equipment

A garage has more than just tools; it has equipment that keeps your whole house working smoothly, including:
- the furnace to keep you both comfortable,
- the hot water heater to keep you both clean,
- the electrical box to keep you both energized,
- the security system to keep you both safe.

This equipment helps your house stay healthy. In some ways they affect every room we've talked about. Your marriage needs strategies to deal with each of these issues.

Furnace Strategies

Every marriage goes through seasons when things get hot and things cool down. You need a way to keep the hot from turning into anger and frustration and to keep the cool from turning into lack of love or ambivalence. A good furnace will regulate the temperature, making every room comfortable for those inside the house. Problems can show up in any room. A hot or a cold draft can start in one room and soon impact every room. You need a furnace system that knows when to heat up and when to turn down. You also need good duct work that flows equally into every room. Hot hallways and cold closets soon throw off the temperature in the bedroom, the kitchen, and everywhere else.

Finding the right temperature for both of you might be a challenge. He might feel most comfortable when it is cooler and she might like it a bit warmer. Yet the more you can communicate, problem solve, and compromise about what is comfortable, the closer you can get to that perfect point where you both can relax. This is where you both feel good about your relationship. Here are a few furnace strategies to help you grow closer.

- Rate your comfort and contentment with each room.
- Listen seriously to your spouse's evaluation of each room.
- If either of you is not satisfied, be willing to make some changes.
- Continue making changes, both common and creative, until both of you feel positive about every room of your relationship.
- Thank God for your contentment but be careful to not take it for granted.

Hot Water Heater Strategies

We all say and do foolish things which can hurt our spouses. It can happen because of our immaturity or selfishness; it can happen accidentally or on purpose. If we could never be forgiven for our mistakes, sins, and failures related to our partners, then every marriage would be doomed. The core of the Christian faith is forgiveness and the opportunity for a second chance. Marriages probably need this more than any other human relationship.

Every house has some combination of shower, sink, and bathtub. These are each fed by a hot water heater which helps clean us up by washing away dirt, odors, and other things we don't want. In a marriage we periodically need to be washed clean so we can start anew. If we cling to our dirt, we are in trouble. If our spouse won't let us get rid of our dirt, our marriage is in trouble.

Forgiveness is like a hot shower, and many of us need one at least once a day. Here are a few hot water heater strategies to keep you both clean.

- Ask forgiveness quickly and sincerely.
- Show your spouse that you are truly remorseful, and develop a plan so it won't happen again.
- Forgive the other person quickly and sincerely.
- Develop a means of accountability if the negative pattern continues.
- Let go of the past so it will not contaminate the future.

Electrical Box Strategies

Certain things energize a relationship and certain things burn it out. For many couples, things like vacation, compliments, lovemaking, gifts, fun, and communication energize the marriage. When the energy is on, couples feel positive about themselves, each other, and the marriage in general. They smile, they shine, and they might even laugh. Yet when the energy is off, everything is dark. They become confused, angry, or scared, and all that was once positive about the relationship passes away.

Without an electrical box there is no power. Most electrical boxes have various circuits that control the flow of power to individual rooms. The lights in one room might go out, while the lights in the rest of the house shine. If the power in a particular room keeps going out, then maybe the circuit is overloaded and an additional one needs to be installed. The more circuits, the more power. When a house starts losing power, you go back to see what has gotten switched off or what needs expansion. If you don't manage your electrical box, you can either have power shortages or your house will burn down. So pay attention to these electrical box strategies.

- Know what energizes and powers your marriage in every room.
- Ask each other what drains the energy from your relationship.
- Increase your energizers and decrease your drainers.
- Celebrate your energizers.
- Watch carefully for drainers and block them as soon as they are found.

Security System Strategies

Your marriage is under attack. Millions of marriages fail every year that could have been saved. Some of the potential dangers to your relationship are internal like unrealistic expectations, abusive anger, and laziness. Some of the threats are external like addictions, financial stress, and sexual temptations. Most of these difficulties have warning signs, yet many of us disregard the warnings or don't see them until it's too late.

One way to protect your house is to have some form of security system. It may be low-tech like making sure your doors and windows are locked, installing outside lights, or getting a dog. Or you might go more high-tech with sensors, motions detectors, and keypads. It's sad that we need to protect our homes from burglars and intruders, but that is simply the way things are. To ignore this danger is to set yourself up for a break-in, physical attack, or damage to your house. A good security system for your marriage might involve the following:

- Make sure your relationship is as strong as possible in every room.
- Talk to each other about potential threats to your marriage, such as inappropriate relationships, sexual temptations, addictive tendencies, unhealthy friends, boredom, financial crises, or distracting priorities.
- Avoid anything that could hurt your relationship with your spouse.
- Recognize and deal with potential threats when they appear small and insignificant.
- Meet with an accountability person, mentor couple, pastor, or counselor on a regular basis to make sure you are adequately protecting your marriage.

When you have these four items in good working order, it helps every aspect of your marriage. When your relationship is comfortable, clean, energized, and safe, then it grows better and better. Yet a strong marriage doesn't get there without a lot of attention and work.

Constant Projects

No house is perfect.

Every house could use some home improvements. No matter how hard I work on my house, there is still more to do.

- The patio needs to be sealed.
- The chandelier in the entryway needs to be dusted.
- The family room carpet needs to be cleaned.
- One of the closet doors needs to be fixed.
- The ceiling of the bathroom needs a fresh coat of paint.

The list is never done. Now don't get me wrong, I love my house. It is currently in pretty good repair, and Tami has done a fantastic job of decorating it. But I realize that trouble can come quickly. There might be hidden problems I am not aware of that suddenly appear. Last week my daughter rushed up to me and exclaimed, "Dad, there are seven bees in the kitchen and I don't know how they got there!" I raced to the rescue, captured the bees, and let them go outside. Then I watched them fly to the roofline right above the kitchen and work themselves through a tiny crack. Suddenly I had one more job added to my list: *Get rid of a bees' nest and seal up the crack in the roofline.*

This is the way it is with every marriage. You would think that being a psychologist, doing seminars on marriage improvement and writing books on relationships would mean I'd have my act together. But I have the same struggles as you do. My marriage is not perfect—just ask Tami. Yet I do work on it every day. I am constantly trying to be a better husband, and Tami is constantly trying to be a better wife. In fact, right now I am writing these words on the beach in Hawaii because Tami completely surprised me with a trip for my birthday. I came home late several nights ago and, with a twinkle in her eye, she said, "You'd better pack. We're catching a plane for Hawaii at 7:15 tomorrow morning."

I was shocked!

But this is just one of the many ways she shows me she loves me. Tami knows that if you constantly work on your marriage, it will get better and better. Our house and our marriage are both so much better today than they were 10 years ago. And I pray they will both be even better 10 years from now.

As a marriage therapist who has worked with thousands of couples, I plead with you to do a regular appraisal of your marriage and together determine what needs to be repaired, remodeled, or cleaned up. Some items you will both easily agree on. With some rooms you might disagree. You might think all is well, but your spouse might want changes. But this is what I'd recommend: If either one of you thinks there needs to be a change, then there needs to be a change. You want a house that is positive and good for both of you. Only one person being satisfied is not good enough. In a healthy marriage, both individuals are happy.

Once you do your appraisal, choose where to begin. Don't try to do it all at once; that will just overwhelm you. Take your marriage one room at a time, starting with the foundation and then moving to the area in the worst shape.

Please don't get distracted about how it got in this condition or whose fault it was. Just roll up your sleeves and start your improvements. As Thomas Jefferson said, "If our house be on fire, without inquiring whether it was fired from within or without, we must try to extinguish it." In other words, "If it's broken, fix it."

As the two of you work together to improve and strengthen your marriage, remember the words of the apostle Paul:

"[I pray] that out of his glorious, unlimited resources he will give you the mighty inner strength of his Holy Spirit. And I pray that Christ will be more and more at home in your hearts, living within you as you trust in him. May your roots go down deep into the soil of God's marvelous love; and may you be able to feel and understand, as all God's children should, how long, how wide, how deep, and how high his love really is. . . by his mighty power at work within us [God] is able to do far more than we would ever dare to ask or even dream of" (Ephesians 3:16-20, TLB).

APPRAISAL CHECKLIST

How Do I Evaluate My House?

Where do I start? Which rooms are in great shape? Which rooms need some immediate attention?

When we don't know where to begin, it is easy to not do anything. Yet that would be a big mistake. Right now, today, this very moment—evaluate your house. An easy way to do this is to walk through the following checklist, peeking into each room, and noting the condition each is in. Once you discover which rooms need work, read the corresponding chapter in this book for ideas about how to make the best repairs. Then do what needs to be done.

In the future, walk through your marriage at least once a year with this checklist, carefully evaluating your needs. There are a lot of things you do, or should do, at least once a year. They include:

- Speak with your physician.
- See your dentist.
- Change the filter on your furnace.
- Tune up your car.
- Check the batteries in your smoke alarm.

Yet your marriage is just as important, maybe even more important, than the items listed above. So do the marriage checkup now and in the future, every single year. You will never regret it.

Remember, anything truly worthwhile must be cared for. If you neglect regular maintenance of your house, your car, your body, and especially your marriage, sooner or later, something will break down. So here is your marriage checklist. Work on it as a couple or do it separately. Either way, it can be a whole lot of fun and save you a great deal of grief.

Appraisal Checklist Instructions

Read through each question, then mark whether you agree or disagree. If you agree with the question, put a checkmark in the space beside the corresponding number on page 224. If you disagree, leave the space blank. When you are finished, add the number of checks horizontally and place that number to the right of the capital letter. Repeat this for all 12 lines.

Now transpose your number to the capital letters on page 225. That will give you a rating for each of the 12 rooms of your marriage. Note that the higher the number, the better you are doing in that room. (See "How to Score Your Ratings" on page 225). Next, mark down your three highest scores and your three lowest scores. Finally, celebrate your high scores and talk about the things you each do to make those areas so successful. Then study your low scores and talk about what you can do to improve those areas.

	Agree	**Disagree**
1. I feel strongly committed to my marriage.	____	____
2. I am aware of my spouse's current emotional state.	____	____
3. We agree on how to manage our finances.	____	____
4. I feel comfortable with all my spouse's close friends.	____	____
5. We know how to relax together.	____	____
6. I know and appreciate my spouse's intellectual strengths.	____	____

	Agree	Disagree
7. We usually handle conflicts quickly, positively, and in a way that we both agree is fair.	——	——
8. Crisis brings us closer.	——	——
9. We regularly appreciate God's creation side by side.	——	——
10. I am satisfied with our sexual relationship.	——	——
11. We have the same vision of what makes up a healthy marriage.	——	——
12. We share similar spiritual values.	——	——
13. I want to grow old with my mate.	——	——
14. We both feel comfortable talking about our feelings.	——	——
15. We work well together.	——	——
16. We have a number of healthy friends with whom we enjoy spending time.	——	——
17. We periodically get away just the two of us.	——	——
18. We enjoy exploring places, interests, and ideas with each other.	——	——

	Agree	Disagree
19. We know how to fight fair.	⸻	⸻
20. We communicate about crises in a way we both feel comfortable with.	⸻	⸻
21. I am willing to appreciate my spouse's taste in music, movies, literature, or any other type of art, even if it isn't the same as mine.	⸻	⸻
22. My spouse is romantic.	⸻	⸻
23. The two of us have talked about our dreams.	⸻	⸻
24. We are both interested in spiritual growth.	⸻	⸻
25. I will never let a person of the opposite sex be more intimate with me than my spouse.	⸻	⸻
26. I can read my spouse's emotions.	⸻	⸻
27. We support each other when it comes to parenting issues.	⸻	⸻
28. My friends encourage my marriage.	⸻	⸻
29. We enjoy spending time together.	⸻	⸻
30. We frequently discuss interesting topics.	⸻	⸻

	Agree	**Disagree**
31. We usually feel closer after an argument than before one.	——	——
32. I commit to stand beside my spouse through any crisis or struggle he or she might battle.	——	——
33. We allow simplicity to draw us closer.	——	——
34. We love to kiss.	——	——
35. We have set individual and relationship goals, and we work together to meet them.	——	——
36. I pray for my spouse daily.	——	——
37. I am committed to not doing anything that would purposely hurt my partner.	——	——
38. I have a sense of those things that emotionally hit or trigger my spouse.	——	——
39. We have certain household tasks that we do side by side.	——	——
40. We get together with good friends on a regular basis.	——	——
41. We laugh together at least once a month.	——	——

	Agree	Disagree
42. We teach each other new things on a regular basis.	———	———
43. I am not afraid to bring up tough topics.	———	———
44. I try to be a servant when my mate experiences physical difficulties.	———	———
45. We take the time to enjoy beautiful things together.	———	———
46. I know what my spouse enjoys sexually and I am willing to put his or her desires above mine.	———	———
47. We meet our goals.	———	———
48. We encourage each other to grow spiritually and know God better.	———	———
49. We are more committed to our marriage than most couples.	———	———
50. We are emotionally tuned-in to each other.	———	———
51. We frequently work together on everyday tasks.	———	———
52. We don't let family or friends get between us.	———	———
53. We know how to have a great time together.	———	———

	Agree	Disagree
54. We are both curious about what the other thinks is interesting.	——	——
55. We don't fight as much as we used to.	——	——
56. We have learned to lean on each other when times are tough.	——	——
57. I talk more about the positives of life than the negatives.	——	——
58. We are more sexually compatible now than we were earlier in our marriage.	——	——
59. I have helped my spouse meet at least one of his or her dreams in the past year.	——	——
60. We regularly serve God by doing things for other people.	——	——

Score Sheet

1 ___	13 ___	25 ___	37 ___	49 ___	A ___
2 ___	14 ___	26 ___	38 ___	50 ___	B ___
3 ___	15 ___	27 ___	39 ___	51 ___	C ___
4 ___	16 ___	28 ___	40 ___	52 ___	D ___
5 ___	17 ___	29 ___	41 ___	53 ___	E ___
6 ___	18 ___	30 ___	42 ___	54 ___	F ___
7 ___	19 ___	31 ___	43 ___	55 ___	G ___
8 ___	20 ___	32 ___	44 ___	56 ___	H ___
9 ___	21 ___	33 ___	45 ___	57 ___	I ___
10 ___	22 ___	34 ___	46 ___	58 ___	J ___
11 ___	23 ___	35 ___	47 ___	59 ___	K ___
12 ___	24 ___	36 ___	48 ___	60 ___	L ___

Rating Sheet

A ___	Commitment Togetherness	(Entryway)
B ___	Emotional Togetherness	(Closets)
C ___	Practical Togetherness	(Kitchen)
D ___	Social Togetherness	(Dining Room)
E ___	Recreational Togetherness	(Family Room)
F ___	Intellectual Togetherness	(Study)
G ___	Conflict Togetherness	(Hallway)
H ___	Crisis Togetherness	(Safe Room)
I ___	Aesthetic Togetherness	(Patio)
J ___	Sexual Togetherness	(Bedroom)
K ___	Future Togetherness	(Addition)
L ___	Spiritual Togetherness	(Foundation)

How to Score Your Ratings

4-5   Doing great
3   Need to clean something up
2   Need to consider remodeling
0-1   Need some repairs

Highest 3 Areas
(These rooms are in great shape.)
1. _____
2. _____
3. _____

Lowest 3 Areas
(These rooms need some work.)
1. _____
2. _____
3. _____

BIBLIOGRAPHY

Arp, David and Claudia. *The Second Half of Marriage*. Grand Rapids, Mich.: Zondervan, 1996.

Button, Mark and Diane. *The Letter Box: A Story of Enduring Love*. Hillsboro, Ore.: Beyond Words Publishing, 2002.

Chapman, Gary. *The Five Love Languages: How to Express Heartfelt Commitment to Your Mate*. Chicago: Northfield Publishers, 1992.

Grigsby, Connie and Nancy Cobb. *How to Get Your Husband to Talk to You*. Sisters, Ore.: Multnomah Press, 2001.

Dobson, James and Shirley. *Night Light: A Devotional for Couples*. Sisters, Ore,: Multnomah Press, 2000.

Harris, Joshua. *Boy Meets Girl: Say Hello to Courtship*. Sisters, Ore.: Multnomah Press, 2000.

Omartian, Stormie. *The Power of a Praying Wife*. Eugene, Ore.: Harvest House Publishers, 1997.

Omartian, Stormie. *The Power of a Praying Husband*. Eugene, Ore,: Harvest House Publishers, 2001.

Parrott, Drs. Les and Leslie. *The Love List*. Grand Rapids, Mich.: Zondervan, 2002.

Rainey, Dennis and Barbara. *Two Hearts Praying as One*. Sisters, Ore,: Multnomah, 2003.

Rosberg, Dr. Gary and Barbara. *The 5 Love Needs of Men and Women*. Wheaton, Ill.: Tyndale House Publishers, 2001.

Sande, Ken. *The Peacemaker: A Biblical Guide to Resolving Personal Conflict*. Grand Rapids, Mich.: Baker Book House, 2004.

Stephens, Steve. *20 Surprisingly Simple Rules and Tools for a Great Marriage*. Wheaton, Ill.: Tyndale Publishers, 2003.

Thomas, Gary L. *Sacred Marriage*. Grand Rapids, Mich.: Zondervan, 2002.

Vanauken, Sheldon. *A Severe Mercy*. San Francisco: Harper and Row, 1987.

Wheat, Dr. Ed and Gloria Okes Perkins. *Lovelife for Every Married Couple*. Grand Rapids, Mich.: Zondervan, 1997.

FOCUS ON THE FAMILY®

Welcome to the family!

Whether you purchased this book, borrowed it, or received it as a gift, we're glad you're reading it. It's just one of the many helpful, encouraging, and biblically based resources produced by Focus on the Family for people in all stages of life.

Focus began in 1977 with the vision of one man, Dr. James Dobson, a licensed psychologist and author of numerous best-selling books on marriage, parenting, and family. Alarmed by the societal, political, and economic pressures that were threatening the existence of the American family, Dr. Dobson founded Focus on the Family with one employee and a once-a-week radio broadcast aired on 36 stations.

Now an international organization reaching millions of people daily, Focus on the Family is dedicated to preserving values and strengthening and encouraging families through the life-changing message of Jesus Christ.

Focus on the Family Magazines

These faith-building, character-developing publications address the interests, issues, concerns, and challenges faced by every member of your family from preschool through the senior years.

| Focus on the Family **Citizen®** U.S. news issues | Focus on the Family **Clubhouse Jr.™** Ages 4 to 8 | Focus on the Family **Clubhouse™** Ages 8 to 12 | **Breakaway®** Teen guys | **Brio®** Teen girls 12 to 16 | **Brio & Beyond®** Teen girls 16 to 19 | **Plugged In®** Reviews movies, music, TV |

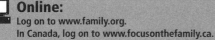

FOR MORE INFORMATION

Online:
Log on to www.family.org.
In Canada, log on to www.focusonthefamily.ca.

Phone:
Call toll free: (800) A-FAMILY (232-6459).
In Canada, call toll free: (800) 661-9800.

BP06XFM

build a
stronger marriage

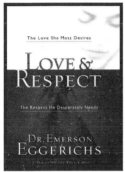

Love & Respect

You can crack the communication code between male and female and reap the benefits of a strong marriage by discovering how love and respect fit hand in glove. Based on extensive research, this book introduces the biblical teaching of unconditional respect — a concept as powerful as unconditional love. This groundbreaking advice offers much-needed help to make your marriage thrive. Hardcover.

The Love List

Drs. Les and Leslie Parrott know that an intentional couple can revolutionize their marriage. *The Love List* presents eight healthy habits that refresh, transform, and restore the intimacy of the marriage relationship. Filled with practical suggestions, this book will help you make daily, weekly, monthly, and yearly improvements in your marriage. Hardcover.

Healing the Hurt in Your Marriage

Do you avoid conflict resolution because you don't know how to deal with it effectively? *Healing the Hurt in Your Marriage* provides you with an excellent examination of conflict and a practical step-by-step process for resolving it in a healthy manner. Refined from over 23,000 hours of private counseling, Dr. Rosberg's unique "closing the loop" technique can help heal hurts, improve communication, foster forgiveness, promote trust, and build a sound marriage. Paperback.

Look for these special books in your local Christian bookstore — or request them from us. Either log on to **www.family.org** or call Focus on the Family toll free at **(800) A-FAMILY (232-6459)**. Friends in Canada can log on to **www.focusonthefamily.ca** or call **(800) 661-9800**. You may also send your request to Focus on the Family, Colorado Springs, CO 80995. In Canada, write to Focus on the Family, PO Box 9800, Stn Terminal, Vancouver, BC V6B 4G3.